A PREFACE TO
RACIAL UNDERSTANDING

BY CHARLES S. JOHNSON

A Preface to
Racial
Understanding

FRIENDSHIP PRESS

NEW YORK

CHARLES S. JOHNSON, Ph.B., Litt.D., has   1928 been
director of the Department of Social Science of   University,
Nashville, Tennessee. He received an A.B. degr   Virginia
Union University and did graduate study in soc   at the
University of Chicago. In 1917, while a graduate   nt, he
served as investigator of Negro migrations for the   negie
Foundation, and organized and became director of   De-
partment of Research and Investigation for the Chicago   an
League. Following the Chicago race riots in 1919, he w
pointed by Governor Lowden as the associate executive,
Graham Romeyn Taylor, for the study of the social and
nomic factors out of which that crisis developed. In 1921
was made head of the research department of the Nation.
Urban League, and later founded its monthly publication,
Opportunity, which he edited until 1928.

Dr. Johnson has also served on several commissions for the
improvement of conditions among Negroes, and in 1929 was
appointed the American member of a League of Nations commission of three to investigate forced labor in Liberia. In 1930
he was awarded the Harmon gold medal for distinguished
achievement among Negroes in science. He has been in charge
of special studies of the Negro population for the Tennessee
Valley Authority and the Division of Review of the National
Recovery Administration. Between 1933 and 1935 Dr. Johnson
made a study of the problems of tenancy in cotton areas, which
contributed to the factual basis on which legislation has been
planned to relieve the plight of the cotton tenant in the South.
In the summer of 1935 he investigated rural social conditions
in Denmark and Ireland.

Dr. Johnson is the author of *The Negro in American Civilization, The Economic Status of the Negro, Shadow of the
Plantation* and several other sociological studies. He is co-author
of *The Negro in Chicago, Race Relations* and *The Collapse of
Cotton Tenancy.*

To the memory of my father

CONTENTS

Contents

Chapter Four

THE EDUCATION OF THE NEGRO
Page 65

Chapter Five

THE CONTRIBUTION OF THE NEGRO TO AMERICAN CIVILIZATION
Page 88

Chapter Six

SOME PORTRAITS OF NEGRO AMERICANS
Page 113

Contents

Chapter Seven

THE NEGRO AND THE CHURCH
Page 140

Chapter Eight

THE CONQUEST OF RACIAL PREJUDICE
Page 160

BIBLIOGRAPHICAL NOTES
Page 193

INDEX
Page 203

A PREFACE TO
RACIAL UNDERSTANDING

CHAPTER ONE

THE STORY OF THE NEGRO

THERE have been two great crises in the history of the Negro race. The first of these followed the contact of Europe with Africa in the fifteenth century, initiating a vast and profitable slave trade which eventually resulted in the bringing of African natives as laborers to the New World. The second followed the partitioning of all Africa, with trivial exceptions, into zones of European influence, when European civilization was carried in forthright earnest to the African natives. These two events are intimately bound up with the course of New World history and with some of the most portentous forces moving in the world today.

THE BACKGROUNDS OF SLAVERY

The movement of black slaves to America was at first a mere incident in the building of a new civilization in a virgin country. The movement of Europe to Africa followed a great missionary enterprise which had as its objective the Christianization of the dark continent. But just as the first was the beginning of an expanding series of incidents which could be neither reversed nor checked, the second became an incongruous prelude to the extension of Europe's world markets, the opening up of vast new sources of raw materials, and the inauguration of an era of imperialism and bitter national rivalries over land and resources which today threaten all European civilization. "The fate of the Negro," said a wise observer seventy years ago, "is the romance of our age."

The history of the Negro, and the equally fascinating history of widely divergent cultures in contact, may be followed in the dispersion of African peoples. Prince Henry of Portugal, when he sailed forth for Africa in the early fifteenth century, had no thought of catching slaves. He was motivated in part by simple adventure, in part by the desire for trade, and in part by the desire to add converts to the holy Roman Catholic Church. Before 1450 he and his companions had reached Senegal; ten years later they had passed the Grain, Ivory and Gold Coasts; and twenty years later they had crossed the equator and traced the entire Congo coast, a stretch of some four thousand miles. The Negroes were curiosities in Portugal as early as 1450, and by 1480 a struggle of nations was in progress, each striving to monopolize for itself a profitable trade in slaves. Portuguese, Spanish, Dutch, English and French traders in turn set up their forts and barracoons along the West Coast of Africa, and there was begun a period of reckless trading in men which lasted for three centuries.

Negro laborers were needed for the New World, and after a halting, uncertain beginning the trade grew to amazing proportions. The first census of the United States, in 1790, showed 697,897 slaves. The demand became so great and the excessive profits stimulated such cupidity that, according to estimates, before slave trading stopped in Africa no fewer than 50,000,000 had been captured. Of these, after the amazingly high mortality of the Middle Passage, at least 10,000,000 were brought to America.

These African natives were commonly regarded as primitive savages, lacking any worth-while social institutions of their own and incapable of absorbing the culture of the Europeans. Early impressions of the Africans in their homes were frequently distorted. Naïve observers, unacquainted with the language, customs and systems of ideas of the new peoples, made judgments on the basis of their own culture and were shocked by practices which they could not understand. It was only natural that the first violent shock of this difference should register in abhorrence of the depravity of the Negro.

There were many African cultures represented among the slaves. The Negro peoples of West Africa, according to Dr. Melville Herskovits, far from being mere savages, came to America out of a sophisticated and highly organized civilization. They had a well developed language, music and art, and a very involved world view. But there was at that time no basis in science for discriminating estimates of unfamiliar cultures.

Under the practical circumstances of life in America many of the original culture traits which belonged to the Africans were sloughed off. No common language could be perpetuated. The wide and promiscuous rehandling of these peoples under a commercial system made unlikely the chances that enough of any one ethnic group would remain together for effective communication. Even without the factor of indiscriminate grouping, it would have been extremely difficult to perpetuate native traits. Few purchasers in the new country could at first afford more than one or two slaves, and soon it became a deliberate policy of purchasers of slaves to separate them at once, as a measure of safety. In the end, many of the distinguishing culture traits disappeared under the necessity for prompt and complete accommodation to the institutions of the New World. Neither the Negro dialect nor the spirituals can be traced definitely to Africa. The Negro speech more closely reflects the eighteenth century speech of Americans than the complex African languages, and the spirituals, based as they are upon the imagery of the Scriptures, are an entirely new product of Negroes in the New World.

Two notable facts may be observed in this connection in explanation of the accommodation of African Negroes to the institution of slavery. A mild domestic slavery was a part of the social organization of many African peoples; and, similarly, there existed among them a profound and deeply embedded respect for the authority of the chief. These old tribal habits, which the anthropologists call intangible culture traits, help to explain how the Negro fell into the pattern of slavery while the Indian, on the other hand, failed to survive its rigors.

Apart from purely cultural factors, the wide variety of strains of alien blood which mingled with the original African

stock added to this cultural alienation a biological one which
is both conspicuous and final. There is no successful precedent
for repatriation among any peoples; and, in view of the vast
changes in Africa and its partitioning among the nations of
Europe, there was no more prospect of return to Africa than
there is present prospect of the return of the descendants of
the early Pilgrim fathers to the mother country.

The first contact of Africans with American culture, curi-
ously enough, was as indentured servants rather than as slaves.
The "twenty Negars" which Captain John Smith records were
landed in Virginia in 1619 by the "Dutch man-o-warre" were
accepted on the same terms as the indentured servants from
England. The adventurous colonists from England, struggling
to bring under cultivation a richly fertile but intractable
wilderness, had a working notion of indenture but not of
slavery. The most striking evidence of the early status of
Negroes in the settlement of the original states is afforded
in a historical court proceeding instituted by a free Negro
who was the first to test in court the flexibility of the indenture provisions. This was the case of Johnson vs. Casor, tried
in 1653, in which it was charged by Casor, a Negro indentured servant, that Johnson was holding him beyond the
stipulated period of indenture. Johnson won, despite important testimony by several leading white citizens who sought
to aid Casor. It was not until years later that the permanent
status of slavery was officially formulated and it was determined by legislation of varying date in the several colonies
just who should be slaves. Significantly enough, the question

was settled first on the grounds of religion rather than of race or color. Thus slavery came to the New World and the Negroes became formally and finally the human content of the institution.

EMERGENCE OF THE NEGRO LABOR PROBLEM

In our present age of mechanical power it is almost inconceivable that there has ever been anything else in robust America than some form of this mechanical power. The foundation of the new country, however, was not machinery but massed and regimented human labor. Negroes supplied at each arduous step the successive staple crops on which the country relied for support. The system of slavery eventually pushed out the free white labor in Virginia and preempted the labor field in the states to the south when cotton plantations began to flourish. It created a class of impoverished non-slaveholding folk known contemptuously by slave owners and slaves alike as "poor whites." The bitter enmities engendered as a result of this struggle must be accounted a part of the present picture of race relations. Finally, the Civil War and subsequent Negro emancipation released these white workers from leisurely strangulation by this system of bound labor.

The white workers actually outnumbered the slaveholders, and, with the wiping away by the war of both capital investment in slaves and prestige alike, there developed a bitter struggle for political power. This battle was waged by the white workers at the same time that they were competing with the newly emancipated Negroes for economic advantage. One result of this new order of things can be observed in the wave of legislation, beginning about 1880, designed to fix the spheres of race contact and relations. A gradual decline in skilled jobs for Negroes followed, and continues even today. So sustained and intense has been the racial sentiment engendered that many white workers and employers now have gone so far as to deny that Negro workers have ever had any notable capacity for skilled work.

In the North, where industries were expanding rapidly toward the end of the nineteenth century, the unskilled work was done by European immigrants. For years, in addition to the increasing economic difficulties in the South, Negroes found no easy entrance to the new industries of the North. Comparatively small numbers already living in that section held personal service positions and battled fitfully among successive immigration waves for unskilled jobs in construction and in the great railway building projects. For the most part Negroes were bottled up ineffectually in the South until an opportunity was provided, during the World War, to fill the places of the immigrants whose services were needed in the fatherlands. Once released, they rushed into the Northern industrial towns like a surging torrent. Before the current of this migration was checked in 1924 over a million and a half Negroes had changed homes, acute tension had been somewhat relieved in parts of the South, and the race problem had been introduced into the states of the North and Northwest.

A Preface to Racial Understanding

STATUS OF THE NEGRO SINCE EMANCIPATION

Interesting as is the economic relationship which has evolved, the present social status of the race deserves next attention. The logic of slavery fixed the Negro's inferior status in America, and this status was passionately defended by science, statecraft and religion. Emancipation swept away the legal status of slavery but could not so easily uproot the mores which were the result of three centuries of development. The Negroes, who had been somewhat protected in the privilege of working (without enjoying the fruits of their labor) and in their health (since like other chattels and cattle they were better workers when sound in body), were thrown precipitantly upon their own resources with no preparation for freedom. They were poor and propertyless, and illiterate. Political demagogues, seizing upon the opportunity to win favor with the emergent white workers, lashed racial antagonisms to fever heat. The economic struggle invaded every corner of social life. The question of the education of Negro children was viewed as a new white man's burden, and funds for education were limited in the belief that the Negroes were incapable of absorbing education and, in their intended status, did not need it even if they were capable.

The disparity in per capita expenditures in white and Negro education continues to this day and may be represented in the average figures of $22.22 for whites and $1.78 for Negroes in counties predominantly Negro, and $11.11 for whites and $3.19 for Negroes in counties from 25 to 50 per cent Negro.

The Story of the Negro

The death rate among Negroes during and immediately after the Reconstruction period mounted to the highest figure since their introduction to America. The number of lynchings was at a high point and was moving to that maximum of an annual average of 166 between the years 1890 and 1900. There was a beginning of the "grandfather clauses" in the suffrage laws and of legislation separating the races in every phase of civic life. Between 1881 and 1907 every Southern state except Missouri enacted legislation requiring that white and colored persons occupy separate seats, compartments or coaches in any vehicle for transportation.

The reduction in Negro mortality from almost three times the white rate to the point at which the white rate stood about twenty years ago, demands a revision of the notion that Negroes are constitutionally doomed to extinction from tuberculosis and the venereal diseases. The present disparity in the death rate of the two races reflects, in part at least, the difference in application of the public health programs and facilities. The inferior economic circumstances of the Negro group, in turn, bear a significant relationship to inadequate housing and artificial restriction on residential areas.

Any summary of Negro status in American civilization is a story of attitudes—of attitudes changing slowly with the steady movement of economic forces. Here we have a civilization born of applied science and invention, of pyramiding industry and technological development, of a new rich country and a new population. The rapid and extensive development of this very structure has given rise to both class and race divisions and has brought the two groups into conflict. Of a total population of 130,000,000, Negroes form about a tenth. The fears which their number and their complexions inspire are registered in laws against intermarriage, however unnecessary, and in customs preventing association. They are registered also in the continued restriction of voting privileges in many areas, and in mass segregation in public accommodations, in education, worship and play.

The effect upon the Negro himself has been unmistakable. It has developed what psychologists call an oppression psychosis, an inescapable sense of inferiority, an attitude of apology, a sense of guilt over the fact of color and its unpopular connotations. It has tended to develop oversensitiveness. Some compensations have been found in race pride, in protective solidarity, in social protest, in a new and distinctive creative expression in literature and art, and in rediscovery of unself-conscious contributions of the mass to music, folklore and the theatre.

A race problem of unwieldy magnitude and without immediate prospect of solution is one of the features of this Negro status in America; it is one of the most significant characteristics of the American scene. However, as has been noted by a student of our national problems, the tendency of the American civilization is toward diffusion of its gains, such as they are. The whole social experiment, in one sense, aims vaguely at raising the level of the mass. The spread of education must carry with it a measure of the values of intellectual and artistic life. The "excessive sociability that breeds conformity" makes us uneasy until our advantages are shared with the less fortunate. And herein lies a measure of hope for the future of the Negro in America. Further hope rests in the self-adjustment of Negroes themselves to the economic and cultural demands of a new period of American development.

EFFECTS OF EUROPEAN EXPANSION IN AFRICA

We have given much attention to the American scene. We must now consider Africa. The first parceling out of that continent was not a casual accident. It came irrevocably and logically from certain economic forces: the need of new markets, the need of new sources of raw materials, and the need of new fields for capital. These very largely determined the fate of millions of natives of Africa. The zeal for the civilizing of backward peoples, which arose in the inevitable conflict of cultures, became confused, as a motive, with an immediate need of their land, their labor and their products. Thus, the latter part of the nineteenth century gave birth to a period of European imperialism which became so intense as to threaten international conflict and to prompt shameful lapses of national ethics in the making of treaties and in all dealings with weaker and less enlightened peoples. In the name of civilization there was inaugurated a period of reckless and heartless land grabbing, subjugation of native peoples to alien law and labor demands, and brutalities and shameless exploitation, culminating in the notorious scandal of the Belgian King Leopold's venture in the Congo basin, which startled the world to its senses.

A Preface to Racial Understanding

Africa, with almost negligible exceptions, now belongs to
Britain, France, Belgium, Portugal, Italy and Spain. In 1877
Stanley opened the Congo basin, with its 8,500,000 Bantu
Negroes, for Belgium, and the scramble for possessions began.
Britain took Nigeria, with its 18,500,000 Negroes, Uganda, and
British East Africa—some 798,000 square miles in all. In one
year, 1884, Germany, under Bismarck, took Togoland, the
Cameroons, and South West Africa, and later annexed
384,180 square miles in East Africa. France added to Senegal
the territories of Dahomey, French Guinea, the Ivory Coast
(with a vast hinterland in Mauretania), and French Sudan—
an empire of 1,078,957 square miles and over 12,000,000
Negroes. With the exception of Germany, which lost its colonies in the World War, each of these countries has in later
years still further enlarged its territory. Italy in 1889 took
Somaliland and was prevented from taking Ethiopia only by
the natural barriers to conquest in its mountains and climate
and by a surprisingly effective resistance by force of arms.
In very recent years the startling logic of imperialism and expansion has appeared in the flagrant flaunting by Italy of all
codes of justice and humanity in its determination to appro-
priate for its own use the land and natural resources of
Ethiopia.

Out of this conflict of cultures has arisen a Negro problem, variously styled the "native problem" and the "white
man's burden." On the one hand it is, as Pitt-Rivers suggests,
the problem of realizing the white man's interest in a black
man's country; and on the other, the Negro's problem of

maintaining his own existence, identity and welfare. Lands have been alienated, new systems of labor instituted, old tribal traditions destroyed, and taxation introduced in the name of civilization. No one may question whether the ultimate aim is humanitarian or economic or both. If European civilization is inevitable, if civilized peoples of the world require the undeveloped resources of Africa, if the backward peoples of Africa require protection against themselves or against one or the other of the European nations, it is also true that the new habits formed demand new goods which the European factories are all too eager to supply.

Colonial policy has been varied. In Kenya, one-half of all the arable land is in the hands of two thousand Europeans, the other half at the disposal of two million natives; there has been forced labor for government work; breach of labor contracts with an employer is a penal offense; independent agricultural production by natives is discouraged. In South Africa the effort, more or less successful, to build European civilization has pushed the natives back from their land upon reserves, demanded their labor, and set up a color bar in industry as well as in social relations which binds them to a hopelessly low economic status. The impact of the new civilization has destroyed the old native economic system, substituted European goods, implanted European standards, altered the productive work of the native household, revolutionized native agriculture, put hundreds of thousands into mines, workshops and roads, and redistributed the native tribes into classes.

A Preface to Racial Understanding

In West Africa, under more enlightened administration, the same general forces have been operating. There has been soul-less regimentation, but with it some attempt, notably by the British, to seek the native's interest. More humanitarian in outlook, this policy is strategic also in its realization that the hope of the future lies in a more enlightened native population. The voluntary efforts of Negro native farmers have been encouraged to the extent that they practically control the cocoa market of the world. The same policy has fostered interest in education. It is realized that when the old culture of the natives has been destroyed it can never again be revived, and that the new culture can be absorbed only if it has indigenous roots. Education in Africa now looks forward to the creation of a new atmosphere of ideas, a self-perpetuating framework of ideas, a new tradition. They go hand in hand with the rising sentiment of solicitude in Europe and America for these long-exploited peoples and a growing concern for the future— a concern that has been stimulated by the menacing unrest of the natives themselves.

DIVERSITY OF THE AMERICAN RACE PROBLEM

It is the custom to refer to the American race problem as if it had always existed and would continue as long as the races are in association. Actually, race problems are comparatively recent in development, and race relations, far from being fixed and unchanging, vary widely throughout the country according to region, economic condition, and special histories of the various groups in contact. For this reason simple generalizations about race problems and relations are likely to obscure their real nature.

There are as many kinds of race relations as there are groups having different backgrounds and experiences, and the population of the United States is conspicuous among the great nations for the diversity of its groups. As historians have pointed out, differences in original stock, emphasized by different geographical conditions and the isolated life of the colonial period, have resulted in important regional differences. This situation can be very clearly observed in the actual course of development of race problems among different American groups.

The first contact of the Negro with the New World was during the explorations of the Portuguese and Spanish. These Latins differed from the English in national habits, temperament and traditions, although in the beginning both sought similar ends in the New World. The difference promptly reflected itself in the relations of the white and black groups in association. Historians of the period of Spanish exploration report with astonishment the frequent appearance of Negroes in incidents of historical importance. These Negroes, it is true, lacked the glamor and grandeur of the priesthood or of the military, but they appear, nevertheless, to have been essential to the success of both the priesthood and the military.

When Balboa discovered the Pacific there was with him Nuflo de Olana, a Negro. Menéndez had a company of trained Negro artisans and agriculturists when he founded St. Augustine in 1565. A Negro accompanied De Soto to Alabama, and, remaining with the Indians, became the first settler of the state from the Old World. Cortez carried Negroes and Indians from Cuba to Mexico, and one of these, Juan Garrido, was the first to plant and reap wheat in Mexico. They were with Ponce de León in his search for the fountain of youth, which resulted in the discovery of Florida. Another Negro, Stephen Dorantes, called Estevan, one of the survivors of a group of six hundred colonists bound from Spain to the New World and disastrously shipwrecked, eventually led a party to the "Seven Cities of Cibola," which are now recognized as New Mexico and Arizona.

Sugar culture in Spain and the Canary Islands was transferred to the West Indies by Negro laborers, and from the West Indies to Louisiana. The historian, Sir Arthur Helps, wrote that when Francisco Pizarro was slain by conspirators, his body was dragged to the cathedral by two Negroes. Negroes were with Lucas Vásquez de Ayllón in 1526 at what is now Jamestown, performing the heaviest portion of the labor, building the first huts, and planting corn. It is estimated that there were no fewer than ten thousand Negroes in the New World as early as 1528.

Negroes were regarded as menial laborers but not as an inferior race, and relations in the New World were influenced very largely by the status of these individuals in the old country. It was possible both in Portugal and in Spain for Negroes to attain to positions of considerable eminence. In 1546 Juan Latino, an African, received an academic degree from the University of Granada in Spain, and later became *Magister*

Latinus at the same university. It was the highest professorship in the royal college. His biographer, Antonio Marin Ocete, in speaking of his work on the Latin grammar, says that "after three centuries the minds of these men [the humanists of Europe] reached the same conclusion as the Spanish grammarians with which in some way or the other Juan Latino was much concerned." Latino's poetry in Latin is preserved today as an example of the most precise and brilliant writing of the early Spanish scholars in this medium. To cite only one other example, there are preserved today in the Convent of the Capuchinos, in the treasury room of the Basilica of Sevilla, and in the Musea Provincial de Sevilla, religious paintings by Sebastian Gómez, an African living in Spain during this period. These paintings, which include the "Immaculate Conception," "The Sacred Family," and "Jesus Tied to a Column," are of such perfection of detail and power of conception as to have been mistaken for over a hundred years for the work of his master, the great Spanish painter, Murillo.

It is thus not surprising that the type of slavery—and later the race relations—which developed in Brazil, where the Latin influence was more prolonged, should assume a widely different pattern from that among the English colonists. Today in Brazil, where there are numerous descendants of the Africans, the race problem is very different from that found in our own South.

Another type of relationship is illustrated by the mingling of the French and the Negroes in Louisiana. There grew up as a result, and there continues to exist, an interesting Negro

society, largely of mixed bloods. Many of these Negroes
in the early period were educated in France, and not a few of
them were slaveholders. They fought with Andrew Jackson
in 1815, and raised a regiment to aid the cause of the Con-
federacy in the Civil War. At that time they were paying taxes
on over fifteen million dollars' worth of property in the city
of New Orleans alone.[1] In 1843 they were publishing in
French a literary magazine, *L'Album Littéraire*, which was
the first of its type by Negroes.

These incidents are not intended to suggest that all Negroes
in Louisiana enjoyed freedom of movement or that Negro in-
tellectuals in America generally were wholly free from the
limitations placed upon them because of their race. There was
the *Code Noir*, which attempted to define relations, but the
code was one of the most humane of the slave codes written
or maintained by custom. It provided for baptism and instruction in the Catholic religion. Concubinage and adultery were
prohibited, but marriage within the church was permitted.
The struggle of France with Spain, and later with the United
States, for the possession of Louisiana no doubt shifted the
focus of attention from racial status.

There was a significant difference in the manner in which
race relations developed among the Latins and among the
Anglo-Saxons. With the Latins an original slave status tended
to be relaxed into servitude and freedom, while under the
Anglo-Saxons Negro servitude gradually tightened into

[1] Henry Clay Wormoth, *War, Politics and Reconstruction*, The Macmillan
Co., New York, 1930, p. 42.

slavery. As indicated earlier in this chapter, slavery as an economic institution was not brought over fully developed by the English into the New World, but took form step by step. Voluntary servitude became involuntary when "legal authority condemned a person to a term of servitude judged necessary for his reformation or prevention from an idle course of life, or as a reprieve from other punishment for misdemeanors already committed." [1] The disposal of white and black indentured servants took the form of sales of persons, even before slavery was crystallized. The assignment of contracts by deed or will followed, and this, in turn, was a legal forerunner of domestic trading in slaves. This practice was applicable to white and Negro servants alike, and it became permissible to assign a servant's contract, with legal sanction, whether the servant gave his consent to such an assignment or not.

During periods of economic stress the selling of unexpired periods of service was widely practised, and as a result, according to Ballagh, "the idea of the contract and of the legal personality of the servant was gradually lost sight of in the disposition to regard him as a chattel and a part of the personal estate of his master, which might be treated and disposed of very much in the same way as the rest of the estate." [2] Later a limit was placed on the absolute right of assignment of contract by excluding "Jews, Moors and Moham-

---

[1] J. C. Ballagh, *White Servitude in the Colony of Virginia,* Johns Hopkins Press, Baltimore, 1895, p. 33.
[2] *Ibid.,* p. 44.

medans" from the privilege because they could not give Christian care and usage. These could not own Christian servants, but they could own non-Christian servants, and many of them did.

ECONOMIC AND SOCIAL ASPECTS OF SLAVERY

The plentifulness and cheapness of land, the impossibility of developing a staple crop with labor bound only for a brief period of years, and the inevitability of losing hired help fixed the logic of slavery. A white servant once away from his master could not be distinguished by his complexion from other whites. He could go west and do for himself what the colonists were using his labor to do for them. But the Negro carried an inescapable livery of his station in his color, and by this quality he was doomed. In 1726, over a hundred years after the coming of the first Negroes, the full powers of control over white servants by masters were relaxed and free reign given by law to Negro slavery.

The economic aspects of race relations are strongly demonstrated in the fluctuations of race sentiment with what we might call the early business cycle. The colonists were hard put to find a way of living until tobacco growing offered promise of lucrative returns. The labor supply from Africa was found well suited to this task and importations increased. Tobacco became the first great American staple.

As slaves became more valuable economically and a fixed status of labor essential, various reasons were assigned for imposing this status. The first justification for insisting upon the fixed status of slavery was that the slaves were pagan, a reason borrowed from medieval days. The obligation to Christianize the heathen, however, brought a threat of economic loss, and there were endless theological and legislative debates over the issue. It was finally decided that Christian instruction should not alter status. The rationalization based upon a backward culture followed, and it was regarded as a boon to the slave to be thus brought to the blessings of civilization.

The earliest American literature on slavery employs arguments based upon what are now regarded merely as cultural differences. There were also attempts to find justification for slavery in the Bible. The early indiscriminate use of white and Negro servants indicates fairly clearly that race played its most important rôle later in the history of the country.

It was the dependence of the country upon staples, however, that threatened several times the economic and political fortunes of the country. After the Revolutionary War tobacco began to decline as a major staple. There was a corresponding decline in the economic value of the slave, and as a result, more attention was given to his social nature. Manumissions were frequent. There was concern over the colonization of the excess black population where they could develop their own institutions and where they would likewise raise no problem of support. Thomas Jefferson wanted to take over vacant Western lands for the purpose. But the country was too exhausted after fighting a war for independence to take the suggestion very seriously. Other suggestions for colonization included Texas, Mexico, Madagascar, the Sandwich Islands, St. Helena and, finally, the west coast of Africa.

The urge to colonization was partially realized in the founding of the colony of Liberia. In the period between the War of Independence and about 1830, serious movements were begun by Negroes themselves and by their friends to overcome the social results of slavery. The first Negro newspaper, *Freedom's Journal,* was launched in 1827 by John Russwurm who, significantly, was the first Negro college graduate, and who later in disillusionment migrated to Liberia. In North Carolina, another full-blooded Negro, John Chavis, who had received an excellent theological education at Princeton under the famous Dr. Witherspoon, preached in white Presbyterian churches and conducted an exclusive academy for the sons of the state's first citizens. One of his graduates became a judge of the state Supreme Court, and another founded an important educational institution.

KING COTTON AND THE NEGRO

It is possible that slavery would have died out from lack of any use for the institution but for the invention in 1793 of the cotton gin. This invention inaugurated, after a few years, one of the most significant periods in the industrial and agricultural development of the country, and linked itself firmly with the industrial revolution in England. It made possible the profitable cultivation of the short-staple variety of cotton, which previously had required tedious labor to pick out seeds by hand. The confluence of favorable factors pre-

24

pared the way for an unprecedented extension of the slave labor system on a profitable basis. The invention of the spinning jenny and the power loom, together with the establishment of the factory system in England, created a clamorous and insistent demand for cotton. Planters who once were anxious to rid themselves of the burden of their slaves suddenly discovered in them the possibility of a vast new wealth. The new staple crop encouraged high hopes for long-deferred riches. Planters indulged in excessive cultivation with an excitement that could be compared to the historic "Mississippi bubble."

Virginia tried to develop cotton in 1820, but the soil and climate were unfavorable. North and South Carolina swiftly came into the field, and new lands were rapidly opened to cultivation. The whole life of the people was profoundly affected, and the status of Negroes was seriously involved in this change. For as their economic value increased, their humanity was again obscured. The more coldly exacting their new rôle, and the more impersonal their relations with their masters became, the greater the temptation of the whole population involved in cotton culture to explain the plight of these slaves as foreordained by their lower nature. Students of political science, notable among whom was Chancellor Dew of William and Mary College, drawing inspiration from Germany and the early ethnologists, supported the lower-status arguments with measured words of scientific proof. A literature developed which provided learned documentation of the innate and unchanging sub-humanity of the blacks.

25

As the production of cotton increased, the price fell, and the seaboard South, feeling the competition of the virgin soils of the Southwest, saw in the protective tariff legislated for the development of Northern manufacturers the real source of her distress. Anti-slavery agitation in the North, where slavery was unprofitable, quieted such humanitarian sentiments as were struggling for expression in the South and provoked the slaveholders to high indignation over the threat of loss of their property in slaves. Books and pamphlets of this period are alive with fiery arguments in justification of slavery, going to extremes which can only be explained by the temper of desperation.

Today slavery is gone, and we have passed from the machine to the power age, but the traditions and sentiments and some of the very arguments which supported the institution at its height linger to confound all efforts at planning for a new day.

Such is the story, briefly, of Africa and the New World and the civilization of the West. Some of the human and personal elements of this great struggle are revealed in the chapters that follow. The perplexing interplay of these elements of contemporary American life has come to be regarded familiarly as the "Negro problem."

CHAPTER TWO

THE NEGRO WORKER

DURING the early years of American colonial development there were no such elaborate labor saving machines as we have today. The vast power resources in electrical energy and steam, which move the giant wheels of industry with sleek and quiet efficiency, were still to be realized. There was but one source of power for this gigantic undertaking of opening up a new continent, and this was man power. It is this fact that gives such immense importance to the coming of the black man to America. Without his labor, massed, multiplied and regimented, the history of the country would have been profoundly different.

This black labor, although crude in the beginning, uninspired and unrewarded, continued for over a hundred years to be the chief support for the country's commercial agriculture. In a similar manner this labor cleared the way for the development of those industries which now symbolize a great new civilization in the Western world. It is an ironic paradox that in the very process of developing the country this labor was making itself less and less essential to it. When

27

the first stages of colonial development were over, and native resourcefulness in invention could freely express itself, man power began to give way to machinery. Thus, in spite of a rapid increase in the population, and in land and resources, proportionately fewer workers were required.

A few familiar examples will help to illustrate this important change. Today only half as many farmers are needed to feed the nation as were required fifty years ago. The harvesting of the 1930 wheat crop would have required twenty million more men forty-five years ago, if they had had to do it without the mechanical aids now available. When we began our cycle of growth one man could saw about a hundred feet of lumber a day, and for the housing of our early families many sawyers and craftsmen were needed. Today one man with a single machine can saw ten thousand feet of lumber a day. A tractor can do the work of eight men with eight horses and plows, and this is revolutionizing agriculture. Once a man could make four hundred and fifty bricks in eight hours; today one good machine can make forty thousand bricks in one hour. Between 1918 and 1926, while manufacturing output increased about twenty-two per cent and agriculture fourteen per cent, nearly two million workers were dropped from farming, manufacturing and railroads as unnecessary.

The early Negro worker is an obscure bit of history, and the present-day Negro worker tends to be regarded, in many quarters, as an industrial problem. It is frequently overlooked that the position of all labor has undergone a vast change, and

The Negro Worker

that Negro labor finds itself in a new position under the double handicap of a class and caste situation.

Negroes form approximately one-tenth of the population and in normal times provide about one-seventh of the workers. Four-fifths of them are in the South, and over a third are in agriculture. If domestic and personal service occupations are added to agriculture, over sixty per cent of all these workers would be accounted for. Since the migration of hundreds of thousands from Southern rural areas to Northern industrial cities, the number of skilled workers has shown a slight increase in the North. But in the South, where Negroes emerged from slavery in possession of many skilled trades, there has been a gradual decline in the number of skilled workers. About three-fourths of the Negro workers are now engaged in work which is classified as unskilled or semi-skilled. The major industries in which they are employed are: the building trades, iron and steel mills, meat slaughtering and packing, and railway car shops.

Negro Workers in Agriculture

In the South, particularly, Negroes have always been an important part of agriculture. Dr. Rupert B. Vance of the University of North Carolina makes a significant comment about their relation to the South. He says: "The expansion westward of the plantation system was due to nothing so much as the unremitting, back-breaking toil of Negro labor gangs."[1]

[1] *Human Geography of the South,* University of North Carolina Press, Chapel Hill, 1935, p. 193.

A Preface to Racial Understanding

In 1860, just before the Civil War, in eight cotton-growing states of the South, 70.3 per cent of all operators were Negroes. But there have been striking changes in the past seventy years. In 1930 Negroes represented only 35 per cent of the farm operators in the cotton belt. In a similar manner the proportion of the Negro working population engaged in agriculture dropped from a half to a third in about thirty years. The Negro agricultural worker has always found difficulties in making his way, and since 1915 these difficulties have been extremely acute.

Back of the migration of Negroes from the South to cities north and south has been a series of misfortunes in agriculture, for which the boll weevil, droughts and a succession of failing crops have been very largely responsible. The financial returns from agriculture, especially in the states in which most of the Negroes live, have not kept pace with the increases in population needs. It has been increasingly difficult for them either to acquire or to retain ownership of farms. This fact is suggested in the census figures, which show increasing rates of tenancy, not only for Negro farmers but for white farmers. In the state of Georgia, for example, Negro farm ownership fell off as much as thirty per cent over the past decade. Throughout the area there have been decreases in Negro ownership and, unfortunately, these decreases have been most serious in the richer and more productive land.

Around the time of the entrance of America into the World War, the cotton states were experiencing great difficulty with that destructive cotton pest, the boll weevil, which laid waste hundreds of thousands of acres of cotton. When complete dependence is placed upon a single cash crop, and this crop fails, the workers are helpless. It was great good fortune, thus, when the industries which sprang up in response to war needs gave promise of absorbing large numbers of these stranded farmers. This touched off the current of migration which did not check itself until over a million and a half Negroes had moved to the North. Even with such a considerable draining off of the excess agricultural population of the rural South, difficulties continued. In the first place, the invasion of the boll weevil had come at a time when there was considerable demand for cotton abroad. There was a sharp increase in cotton prices as a result of this demand. In 1920 and again in 1924-25, with a larger acreage, the price fell, however. Then, in 1929 there was a destruction of almost one-third of the cotton crop by the boll weevil, and three years later an equally disastrous oversupply of cotton, which forced prices down to a level below the cost of production.

With such dismal uncertainty and with the accumulation of such losses, the South was in a very serious economic plight before the nation-wide depression began to be felt. The European war had temporarily suspended cotton-growing activities in many countries, increasing the demand for American cotton. With the return of peace times our export market began to feel the effects of competition from world markets. Some countries, like England and Russia, for example, have since the war made strenuous efforts to reduce their demand for American cotton, by stimulating cotton growing within their own territories. All of this had its effect upon areas of the South which had depended upon cotton as an export crop.

The great bulk of the Negroes live in the Southeastern states. It is becoming increasingly evident that cotton, the chief commercial crop of this area, can no longer hold its position of importance as a source of cash and subsistence. As a matter of fact, the best cotton areas now appear to be in the Southwest, where the land is more fertile and the topography lends itself more readily to the use of labor saving machinery. Experts concede that Texas and Oklahoma alone, if adequately developed through technical means now perfected and in use in some places, could produce all the cotton needed for the domestic market, and satisfy the present world demand for American cotton. But there are relatively few Negro farmers in these newer cotton areas. This does not augur well for the future unless some steps are taken soon to make fundamental corrections in the present organization of agriculture in the area.

The situation of the Negro worker in agriculture tends to reflect the state of Southern agriculture generally. It is frequently assumed that because Negro workers are now and have been in the past prominently identified with the chief crops of the South, they are responsible for the ills that have overtaken the area. This would be a justifiable assumption if more of the Negro farmers were free to do what they pleased with the land and the crops they tilled. But, first as slaves and later as tenants, they have merely carried out orders. Where they owned their land, even in less fertile areas, they have taken better care of it.

Other factors which have contributed to the present state of agriculture, however, have affected owners as well as tenants. The involved credit system, which supports commercial agriculture, places most serious risks upon the owners. The tenants themselves become a risk in the vicious cycle of low income, low standards and low incentive to improvement. The wholesale loss of farms throughout the South bears eloquent testimony to the unrelenting pressure of a defective system of agriculture upon owners and tenants alike. The great tragedy lies in the perpetuation, through this system, of a hopeless, helpless peasantry which is a burden upon the whole area.

THE PLIGHT OF THE COTTON TENANT

There are 698,839 Negro tenant families in the cotton states alone, and these represent nearly three million individuals. For years it has been vaguely sensed that these were workers of low income and, consequently, of low standards, but they have never commanded very serious attention. Occasional references to them have usually described them as contented, even happy. There is a considerable concern at present over tenants and share croppers generally, because it has suddenly been discovered that this condition is no longer a peculiar problem of the Negro. The country is being made aware that there has grown up, almost without being observed, a population of white tenants who share the evils of a system which grew directly out of the plantation structure under slavery.

A Preface to Racial Understanding

While the situation is a distressing one for the white tenants, the Negroes carry the added weight of a race and slavery tradition. It must be clear to anyone who gives a moment's thought to these lowly workers that no section can improve its agriculture or its civilization until the social and economic level of the lowliest group has been raised.

Not so long ago the writer had an opportunity to study with a fair degree of intimateness the life of a rural Negro group living in the shadow of the plantation.[1] Here was a stagnant peasantry, muffled in a vast apathy, dull and wantless. Year after year life was a succession of disillusionments. Four-fifths of them made no money, their homes were dismal two and three room cabins which failed to offer protection against either the summer rains or the biting breath of winter. Held strictly to the pattern of brute utility by an overwhelming tradition, they shared none of the elements of an enlightened social life; they had to make their own life without the benefit of an inspiring heritage, or of freedom of movement, or of education, or of any sense of social and community responsibility. Here were the true forgotten men of the twentieth century.

The observations made by the writer have since been overwhelmingly supported by others whose attention has been attracted to the plight of these families in other sections. In 1934 Dr. Harold Hoffsommer, of the Alabama Polytechnic Institute, studied 2,000 Alabama cotton share tenants and

[1] The results of this study have been published in *Shadow of the Plantation*, by Charles S. Johnson. University of Chicago Press, 1934. $2.50.

34

found that only 25 per cent of their total years of farming had resulted in any profit whatever. The study of some 2,000 tenant families, in counties of five different states, by the Committee on Minority Groups in the Economic Recovery revealed that during 1934 the actual earnings of these families averaged about $105 a year, or a monthly income of $1.75 for each person. With such earnings it is to be expected that the standard of living would be low; that food would be reduced to pellagra-inducing scarcity and monotony; that the housing would be cramped, dreary and bare; that mortality would be high and family life on a low plane. As a result of the system in which the tenant families live and work there is a dependent and ignorant peasantry, too listless and too harrassed to adjust itself, without aid, to the new requirements of American agriculture.

For those unfamiliar with the system of share tenancy as it is in practice in the cotton belt, some of the major features might be explained. In theory the landlord provides the land, and the tenant provides the labor, and when the crop is raised it is divided between them. The amount of the crop that goes to the landlord, however, depends upon the amount of other essentials provided to the tenant. Thus there are half-, fourth- and third-share tenants, and below these the share croppers, who have almost nothing to offer but their labor.

Tenants rarely have, or can net, enough cash money to support themselves over a crop year, and thus must have credit. This is provided by the landlord in the form of "furnishing." The common articles of the diet—fat meat, corn and molasses

—and items of clothing, are advanced along with the cabin. When the crop is raised the landlord's share of the crop is taken. This is seldom less than half. Then the landlord collects for the advances, to which he adds a flat interest rate and special credit charges, which are reckoned as a sort of security against losses and as compensation for the trouble of keeping the accounts. These costs, by actual examination in a number of states as recently as 1934, averaged for the tenant from thirty to fifty per cent per annum. The landlord keeps the books and his records and assessments, by tradition, are not to be questioned. The results of the practice are most apparent in the preponderant numbers who end their years in debt, and in the increasing numbers of small and insecure farmers who fall back into the tenant class, after resorting to credit.

Seventy years of this system should have been sufficient to reveal those internal weaknesses which threaten the owners as well as their dependent tenants. The recurrent crop failures, the uncertainty of cotton prices, the accumulating areas of exhausted and now valueless land, the loss of farms to the banks and credit agencies, and the constant poverty, should have by now suggested the need of some fundamental change in the agrarian policy of the area.

When cotton was most profitable the United States virtually controlled the cotton market of the world. Other nations now produce much of the cotton which world industry requires. The spread of mechanization is proving devastating to the labor in cotton. With machinery, cotton can be more cheaply produced and with fewer hands. Over all this gloomy prospect impends the perfection of an invention for picking cotton which, even in its present state of development, can without very high capital cost do in seven and a half hours the labor of a good picker working three and a half months.

One need only observe the disastrous results on the tenants of the frantic efforts of the Agricultural Adjustment Administration to aid agriculture, to understand their present position. The vast sums poured into the South to save cotton prices gave a temporary and highly artificial relief by rewarding crop destruction and limitation in the face of need. In the process of aiding the farmers many of the risks of ownership were transferred to the already overburdened tenant. Revisions in the AAA program attempted to correct some of the most serious evils, but it has been impossible to reach the source of these problems under the present structure of agriculture. The Supreme Court decision which declared provisions of this act unconstitutional made necessary a shift of emphasis, in the effort even to control production. The new efforts to aid the farmer, based upon soil conservation, seem to offer less opportunity to help the tenant than the earlier Agricultural Adjustment Act.

Obviously such backwardness is not consistent with the American ideal or with any progressive rural civilization. Practically every civilized country of the world except the United States has undertaken fundamental reforms in its system of land tenure. It is imperative that some reorganization of cotton tenancy be effected now that will provide a decent, self-supporting way of life.

NEGRO WORKERS IN INDUSTRY

Since the migration of over a million and a half of the Negro population from areas throughout the South to points in the North where large basic industries are located, many of them are appearing in manufacturing and transportation fields. There has really never been a time when the cities of the South have not made use of fairly large numbers of Negro workers, and there have been many Negro workers who have performed skilled work. This has been notably true in the building trades.

Two important factors in the recent changes in the economic status of the Negro have been: (a) the migration of the surplus farm populations to towns and cities; and (b) the natural increase in the number of industries which can absorb the excess population. The new situation created has bred competition for work along racial lines. The so-called "Negro jobs" have been invaded by white workers made willing by their depressed circumstances to overlook the social stigma of performing work commonly done by Negroes. But while white workers have been able to move downward into "Negro jobs" rather freely, there has been no similar movement of Negroes upward into "white jobs."

There is just one outstanding advantage which the Negro workers have in the group competition, and this is not a wholly commendable one. Their presence and availability for some of the work being performed by whites, whether they are actually employed or not, operates as a control on wages and on the organization and solidarity of labor and upon its demands for improved wages. This state of affairs has been noted both in the North and in the South. The entrance of these Negro workers shortly after the World War into such large industries of the North as steel, railway maintenance, slaughtering and meat packing—industries once preempted by foreign born laborers—was facilitated by their willingness to accept wages lower than those demanded by organized labor, or even by some unorganized workers longer established in these fields.

The work of Negroes in industry, on the whole, has been confined to the unskilled branches of industry. Perhaps seventy-five per cent of them fall within this classification. The unskilled branches of work have been those most readily affected by seasonal fluctuations and technological improvements. Whereas, in the Northern states, prior to 1914, this unskilled work was done almost entirely by European immigrants, in the South, where there were few industries and fewer immigrants, much of the unskilled work in the cities was done by Negroes. Changes in the occupational adjustment of white and Negro workers, however, had begun long before the general depression in industry. As early as 1880 it could be observed in the occupational statistics that white workers were increasing their proportions in the skilled work of the building trades, in which Negroes formerly held important positions. The vast textile industry, the one outstanding industry in the South, drew all of its labor, except for such menial tasks as cleaning and trucking, from among the rural whites. Jobs which were in the range of political patronage, including such unattractive ones as scavenger and garbage collector, and jobs which might have been considered, from the character of the work, as "Negro jobs," became, increasingly, jobs for unskilled whites who were potentially voters. Barber shops and other types of public personal service operated by Negroes for white patronage began to decline in numbers.

Prior to the World War white women, particularly in the South, did not seek industrial positions, however greatly work was needed, because it involved, to some extent, a loss of status. Since the war they have been increasingly seeking such positions, and are preferred to Negro women for types of work involving the use of machinery. Moreover, they can perform at lower labor cost many jobs which would normally be done by either white or Negro men.

A survey of the position of Negro workers since 1890 would reveal that, with respect to skilled crafts, they have gained slightly in masonry, iron working and stationary engineering, and have lost numbers relatively in carpentry, plastering, brick and tile making, boot and shoe making, blacksmithing, marble and stone cutting, leather currying and tanning.

Between the insecurity of agriculture (largely cotton cultivation) and the fluctuations of unskilled industrial employment, the position of Negro workers has been a most uncertain one. Some indication of this is to be found in the figures

The Negro Worker

for relief and unemployment by race. Although the Negroes constitute 9.7 per cent of the population, they have formed 18.2 per cent of the persons on the relief rolls. But although these unemployment rates are excessively high, and there is a serious situation generally with respect to low wages, at least as many workers are employed as are unemployed.

INDUSTRIAL EFFICIENCY

One of the first questions asked about Negro labor is, "How efficient is it?" The implication is that lack of industrial opportunity is a matter of lack of skill or ability to learn skills. It has been mentioned elsewhere in this volume that Negro workers have demonstrated a capacity for skill by actually performing skilled work successfully. Although differences have been noted between white and Negro workers in efficiency in machine work, this has been due in large part to the initial unfamiliarity of many of the latter with the machines. Where opportunity has been provided for acquiring skill they have proved satisfactory workers. The questioning of employers regarding their opinions about Negro efficiency has drawn difference of views, but the preponderant majority have indicated that they regard Negroes as being equal in efficiency to the corresponding group of white workers.

During the World War emergency, when labor was taxed to its utmost, these workers established records for output difficult to exceed. Perhaps as good evidence as any of their skill is the fact that the Ford automobile plant in Detroit, one of the most efficient industrial organizations in the country, has employed as many as seventeen thousand, keeps a fairly high proportion in its working force, and used a Negro demonstrator for the precision machine which they exhibited at the recent World's Fair in Chicago. This plant is mentioned because it has been conspicuous in other ways for its independence of certain of the traditions of industry.

The transition from agricultural to industrial work for men, and from domestic service to light manufacturing for women has involved the serious questions of new skills and working habits. This was conspicuous during the Negro migrations in 1916-18. For some it was a difficult adjustment; others, and especially those who were permitted a more sustained period of exposure to the exacting speed and precision of industry, found adjustment easy and normal. Problems of adjustment still appear, and these are seriously complicated by the fact that experience with an inefficient Negro is likely to be regarded not as an individual but as a group matter. With white workers, on the other hand, there is no such general racial judgment if one individual or a large chance selection of them turns out to be below standard.

NEGRO WORKERS AND ORGANIZED LABOR

The displaced Negro farm laborers had to seek work in industry because there was nowhere else to turn, and the first real opportunity which came during the World War brought serious problems later. Their use was opposed by labor organizations. This could be understood as long as labor sought to preserve its standards by opposing the use of workers at lower than the union scale. But many of these organizations refused to admit Negro workers when they sought to conform to labor policy, or else they required that the new Negro workers take their chances on jobs and security in separate organizations. Several international organizations, notably the mine workers, longshoremen, and the garment workers, were more liberal in policy and found these workers dependable allies. Certain other unions, while not refusing them, yet did not encourage their membership. The greatest aid to their acceptance by the unions has been the fact that, as non-union workers, they could successfully break any strike which the unions could call.

In 1927 there were as many as fifty thousand Negroes in labor organizations. There was not, however, much incentive to them to continue paying union dues when the locals offered so little protection. Nor was there very much opportunity for learning, in the separate locals, about the principles of labor organizations and strategy. Greater security for most of them rested with the employers, and so interest has continued divided. Much of the difficulty traces back to the influence of the "economy of scarcity" principle in labor, which corresponds to the general industrial policy, now much criticized, of limiting the production of essentials in order to adjust the price level. The craft organization of labor has encouraged the principle of restriction of numbers. However, the recent separation from the American Federation of Labor of a very considerable group under John L. Lewis, head of the United Mine Workers, has initiated a rival movement for industrial organization across craft lines. This form of organization, inasmuch as it escapes the old exclusive policies of the craft unions, is regarded with greater hope by Negro workers.

WORKERS AND THE GOVERNMENT

The problem of unemployment is a serious one generally, and broad measures have been required for recovery. The heavy burden of unemployment for workers in the so-called marginal fields works an especial hardship upon Negroes. The great volume of their work, through no fault or desire of their own, happens to be in the marginal fields. Where workers are to be laid off, the reductions begin in the unskilled ranks and the numbers affected, as a rule, are greater than for other grades of work. When agricultural lands are to be retired for crop reduction purposes, the superfluous tenants must go. When the income of the reasonably well-off family is reduced, it dispenses with a servant. The results, though diffused and quiet, are devastating for the Negro worker. It explains why there are twice as many, proportionately, on the relief rolls. In 1933 there were over two million Negroes receiving relief, and in 1935 it was estimated that close to four million, or about thirty per cent of the Negro population, were receiving relief.

The government programs have attempted seriously to help this group, and when they have failed it has been in large part due to the persistence of old racial customs and practices in local areas. It is noteworthy that in the slum clearance programs, which provided for unskilled and skilled work, it was stipulated in the contracts that Negro workers should be employed up to their proportion of the workers in the population. Although in government jobs, as in private business, Negro workers have been limited with respect to skilled opportunities, they have shared employment in the Tennessee Valley Authority program, the CCC camps, and in the Public and Civil Works Administrations. There has been attached to the Department of the Interior an adviser on Negro affairs, whose duty has been to keep the various departments of the government aware of the special needs of the Negro group, and to aid in securing for them the services offered by the government. Similar advisers are attached to the Departments of Labor and Commerce.

What Can Be Done about It?

The situation of the Negro worker in normal times is by no means secure, and in abnormal times it becomes exceedingly depressing. So many of the acute social problems rest upon this base that it is next to futile to expect permanent improvement without raising materially this economic level. It is important to recognize that the fate of the Negro laborer is closely linked with that of workers generally and with the welfare and prosperity of the country as a whole. Little fundamental improvement in buying power, for example, is possible if through idle whim or misguided racial policy a great bulk of American labor is kept idle or impoverished.

With respect to agriculture, the most hopeful prospect rests upon security of possession of the land, with an opportunity for subsistence and additional cash earnings from produce or labor. Fortunately there has been begun an attempt to remedy the situation of the tenant and small farm owner through the creation of a special federal agency. The sole purpose of this program is the resettlement of share croppers and tenants in the cotton belt, with aid to their ownership of the land, and protection of this ownership from stronger interests. Such a program soundly supported and carried out should mean the beginning of rehabilitation of some seven hundred thousand Negro tenant families, and the relaxing of a terrific even though fruitless pressure of stranded populations in the city.

Various private organizations concerned with labor and with these special Negro problems have sought to find some means of relieving their plight. The activities of the Federal Council of Churches and of the individual churches in picturing the true conditions to the public, counseling correction, and pointing a way to social justice for these unfortunate victims of a reckless age, are bases for future building.

It seems clear that the Negro worker in industry should cast his lot with labor generally, and be encouraged in doing so. Such an association of interests should help to develop a more intelligent and cooperative body of labor, reduce the self-destructive conflict and competition between white and black labor, and raise the living level of all workers. What seems most desirable generally is a readjustment of our entire economic system to the original conception of democracy, and it can well be one of the social missions of the church to see that this ideal is realized in fact.

CHAPTER THREE

SOCIAL FACTORS IN NEGRO LIFE

IT is not enough merely to record social conditions among the Negro population. Everyone who has observed the external aspects of Negro life in our cities knows that they live under serious disabilities, both economic and social, and that these disabilities reflect themselves in low incomes, poor housing, disorganization in home life, and high death and sickness rates. The figures for these rates are both impressive and alarming. What is most necessary now, it seems, is to understand the nature of these disabilities, as a first intelligent step toward doing something about them. This chapter will concern itself chiefly with certain of the fundamental issues regarded as important to an understanding of the social problems which affect the life and wholesome development of the Negro population. These will be limited to consideration of health, housing and the family.

Negro Health as a Social Problem

Mortality statistics reveal, for the country as a whole, a Negro rate nearly ninety per cent greater than the white in

47

urban areas, and fifty per cent greater in rural areas. The highest urban death rates are in the South and the highest rural rates are in the North. The diseases which, authorities agree, are due largely to unfavorable sanitary conditions and low economic status, are responsible for the great disparity between Negro and white rates. These diseases are pulmonary tuberculosis, typhoid, malaria, pellagra, and illness resulting from improper care during childbirth. The highest death rates from tuberculosis among Negroes will be found in much younger age periods than among whites. The rate among Negro boys and girls is six times as high as among white boys and girls. Control of tuberculosis alone, it is estimated, would increase the Negro life span by five years.

According to the Metropolitan Life Insurance Company figures, the Negro tuberculosis death rate is about three times that of the white. If we accept the estimate of the prevalence of tuberculosis made on the basis of a careful and controlled experiment in Framingham, Massachusetts, there are 4 cases of tuberculosis for every 100 Negroes, or approximately 440,000 Negroes in the United States who are ill at all times with the disease. Of this number about four-fifths, or approximately 350,000, live in the South. In spite of the fact that many Negro groups cannot be reached, for one reason or another, by planned public health programs, during the past thirty years they have shared many of the benefits from such general measures as water purification, vaccination, the pasteurization of milk and general economic improvement. Always, however, the lag in mortality decline has persisted.

Social Factors in Negro Life

At one time the very wide difference in white and Negro sickness and mortality rates was thought to be due to some obscure biological difference which could not be reached by ordinary methods of treatment and prevention. The new public health interest has more recently been based on the assumption that many diseases are social and economic in foundation. As a result, important changes have been noted. Little study is necessary to reveal that the mortality rate of the Negro population, considered as a whole, corresponds closely to the mortality rate of any low-income group. Negroes, with largest numbers of their population in the low-income brackets, would thus be expected to have high tuberculosis rates.

A study made in Cincinnati by Dr. Floyd P. Allen [1] indicates that it is actually possible to get a very different racial emphasis when mortality rates from tuberculosis are compared for low-income white groups and high-income Negro groups. The economic factor is the matrix of an expanding series of social problems, from poor housing to inadequate diet; from physical congestion to insufficient hospitalization.

It has always been difficult for the Negro sick to secure anything approaching adequate hospital care. One reason given has been the expense of building separate hospitals. But such institutions really need not be separate. The insensitiveness to physical distress so marked in the policies of excluding Negroes from these institutions can, at times, stir considerable

[1] "Physical Impairment among One Thousand Negro Workers," *American Journal of Public Health and the Nation's Health*. Vol. XXII, June, 1932.

righteous indignation, but the practice continues with tacit public support. The death rate from hospitalized Negro cases of tuberculosis is extremely high, and physicians explain that this is largely due to the fact that they get into the few available places too late for effective aid. The Negro wings of publicly supported hospital buildings are usually inadequate in size, equipment and service. Negro physicians find it virtually impossible to serve their patients in them. The notorious exclusion policies were recently dramatized when Miss Juliette Derricotte, Dean of Women of Fisk University, and a nationally known and loved young woman, died needlessly, following an accident a few blocks from a Georgia hospital. Before she could be treated it was necessary to secure an undertaker's ambulance from a city forty miles away to carry her back to that city.

There is, in the country as a whole, one bed for every one hundred and fifty of the white population and one for every two thousand of the Negro population. And this, despite the fact that the Negroes are much more seriously in need of the attention.

There are factors in the present problem of Negro mortality over which the Negroes themselves have no control, and about which they can do little or nothing. Apart from the yet undetermined influence of racial heredity and the medical opinion regarding special racial immunity and susceptibility to certain diseases, most of the situations imposing hardships and limitations upon the Negroes are social and cultural. In a broad sense, this population's health is dependent upon community mores, stimulated by race difference, which restrict for them the range of occupations, and consequently the level of income.

Such essentials to health as adequate sanitation, water supply and the like, the provision of which is a function of government, can scarcely be brought about by Negroes without a free and intelligent use of the franchise. If we may judge from the all too common tendency of cities to neglect those areas in which politically impotent members of the community live, these residents may expect but little consideration. Indeed, few, if any, of the social restrictions resulting from present race relations can be altered by Negroes alone; unless, perhaps, they can win sympathy or concern over the years by a display of patience in the midst of a rapid wasting of their numbers from curable or preventable diseases.

There are, however, certain elements of the health problem which are modifiable by the Negroes themselves. While it is impossible for them to control the range of their income and their occupation, there are certain groups of individuals within almost every income level who have some margin of resources with which to attack these problems. Not all persons of low income are destroyed by disease, and not all of the survivors are endowed with special immunity. We may assume, therefore, that among certain groups of Negroes there is sufficient awareness of the value of cleanliness, regular habits, avoidance of contagion, and rational expenditure of the family budget, to counteract the invasion of dangerous diseases. Homes may be modest but comfortable, clean, and beautiful.

These are mass measures which reflect the cultural development of the groups involved.

The part that habit and custom play is tremendous; changes come slowly, however much observers may regard these changes as necessary or broadly possible. A vital contribution of Negroes to the solution of their own health problems is possible, but only through the development of an intelligent leadership in social health programs by Negroes themselves.

In this case, as in others, it is never safe to generalize about the Negro race as a whole. There is no single homogeneous Negro group. Education, experience, and contacts have shaped the circumstances of various groups in widely different ways. The largest group may be classified as naïve folk whose social information and habits fall dismally short of modern notions of health standards. In this group we see preserved the folkways and superstitions of Americans of an earlier period. There is a sturdiness of belief in the efficacy of herbs, mole's feet, mare's milk, kerosene, "hands," and, more recently, patent medicines. It is not enough to say merely that they are ignorant or backward or should know better. They must be taught.

There is another large group just emerging from virtual peasantry and facing the new problems of city life. The toll of life among these restless adventurers is tragic and enormous. In the new setting, new standards slowly infiltrate, but with all the waste of the process of learning the ways of the city. There is, finally and more hopefully, a group who have absorbed the new standards and become, to a large extent, aware of the associated values. It is among this group that there is to be found superior education, and it is from them that there should be expected a greater measure of leadership for their own race.

The improvement of Negro health is a racial problem only in so far as public opinion and customary practices have limited ordinary health measures because of race. It is a responsibility of the Negroes to become active agents in this improvement for their own as well as for their neighbor's preservation. But, ultimately, Negro health is a national social problem, and the final responsibility for improvement lies with those individuals and agencies, governmental and private, upon which the nation relies for its guiding principles and for leadership.

HOUSING AS A SOCIAL PROBLEM

A visit to the Negro district of almost any American city is likely to leave an unpleasant memory. The dreary dilapidation of the dwellings, the neglect of the streets, the absence of pavements, the long accumulation of waste, the congestion, and the casual disorder of the shops provoke unsavory pictures of the people. One reason why the area appears to represent so large a part of the Negro population is that those Negro families which escape from it lose their racial label in the general housing picture of the city. But such escape usually is a difficult feat.

The residence sites of Negroes will almost invariably be found near the center of the city, in the oldest residence areas, where buildings are out of date, run down, difficult to keep in repair, and practically impossible of sale because the area has only a limited residence value. The land, on the other hand, is potentially valuable for business, its tax rate is high, and its value is usually beyond the purchasing power of the economic class which occupies the buildings. It is impracticable for investors to build new houses in the area, to repair the houses which are already there, or to do anything that will increase the cost of maintaining them while the maturity of these values is being awaited. When Negroes move in as the last class to occupy them, the rentals tend to increase because, being less desirable as a group than a white group of somewhat lower economic status, they are expected to pay more for the privilege of occupancy. This situation, in which there is observed a confusion of racial and economic factors, contributes to many of the city's problems of congestion and property deterioration, of health and morals.

It is difficult to generalize upon Negro housing because the types of the segregated areas vary so widely. However, Negro sections as a rule have certain definite characteristics: the artificial limitation of the areas; the enforced association of all types and classes of Negro individuals; the tendency to municipal neglect of sections abandoned to Negro residence; the lack of strict enforcement of sanitary regulations; the absence of modern equipment such as bathtubs and running water; the neglect of garbage; and the consequent and frequently original indifference of Negroes themselves to these unfavorable conditions.

Housing, like health, depends to a large extent upon income. It is peculiar to the Negro, however, that even the ability to pay for a better home cannot make one possible because of the disposition of the public to limit residence areas for him. The chronic predicament has had one advantage: the first of the vast slum clearance projects and low-cost housing begun by the federal government was a Negro area in Atlanta, Georgia. This was followed by similar projects in Nashville, Tennessee; Cleveland, Ohio; and in New York City. The outstanding success of the Paul Laurence Dunbar Apartments for Negroes in New York, erected by Mr. John D. Rockefeller, Jr., and the Boulevard Garden Apartments in Chicago, built by Mr. Julius Rosenwald, undoubtedly gave to this venture the assurance of a safe financial, as well as a salutary, social investment.

The Negro Family

The problems of the Negro family in cities are not merely social; they are cultural in a broad and significant sense. It is one thing to record with alarm or with a disparaging tolerance the frequency of desertion, illegitimacy, crime and mortality. It is quite another thing to interpret these as an essential phase of the transition of a group from one basis of social organization to another, or rather from one cultural plane to another.

To know the Negro family as it is today, it is necessary to know its background, that is, the peculiar institutions and customs which have made it what it is. The problems which have developed under the impact of new conditions of life have a very special history. The low economic status of the Negro population accentuates all these social problems, keeps the group isolated from a large measure of participation in general social progress, and adds to the issue of race—which is serious enough—the pressing issue of class.

No discriminating treatment of the Negro in America could fail to take into account the wide cultural differences existing among Negroes in America today. These cultural differences, it is now evident, are not a matter of modifications of an African culture, which none of them retain. They represent progressive stages of adjustment to the accepted American standard. In this sense the adjustment is no different from that experienced by other groups within the American culture who are affected by the same external factors of isolation and local and regional institutions and codes.

Until recently Negroes have been largely a rural people. Most rural people represent a certain type of social isolation. Circumstances have prompted migration to cities both in the South and in the North. This migration has resulted in a serious crisis in Negro life and progress. For the most part, the problems of adjustment observed in the cities have their origin in the rural Southern life and culture.

In tracing some of these problems to their source we have the advantage of an intimate study of several rural areas, the most notable of which, for purposes of contrast, is a plantation area in Alabama.[1] The area in question is one

[1] Charles S. Johnson, *Shadow of the Plantation*.

devoted extensively and almost exclusively to cotton cultivation and in this activity, which dominates the life of the group, there has been retained, with only slight modifications, most of the features of the cotton plantation under the institution of slavery. The population is over eighty per cent Negro, the few white inhabitants being for the most part proprietors or their representatives. Such an area permits us to observe today both the earlier stages of a historical process which began with the transition of the group from slavery, and the present source of migration to the cities.

In the first place, there are not very wide differences in the conditions of the Negroes in the area. Most of them are tenants who have lived in the area most of their lives, and they are isolated. This separation from the general channels is fostered by a high degree of illiteracy, which shields them from the influence of those cultural devices by which social changes are introduced. What is most significant, however, is the fact that there exists in the social consciousness of this group and in its social life, a degree of internal cohesiveness and stability which does not seem to be based upon either African or European culture as much as it is based upon the practical necessities of their peculiar status and rôle in the early American social system.

The general organization of life under the régime of slavery was and had to be—as is the case in all cultures—an organization which permitted the most satisfying functioning of individuals in their setting. Viewed in this light, marriage, the relation of parents to children, divorce, extra-marital relations, illegitimacy, religion, and behavior in emotional crises involving love and death, take on a new significance and value.

Let us note some of the actual points of difference between this pattern of life and that of the familiar American family. In the structure of the American family the father, mother, and their own children form a unit, with the father as head and the chief authority. The family unit is supported by the institution of marriage, and strict social codes govern questions of legitimacy, respectability and morals. In the Negro families living under the conditions described, this pattern is not the rule. This does not mean that the families are indiscriminate groupings, or that they do not have controlling social codes which determine for them what is respectable and what is moral. Nor are the social codes by which they live imposed from the outside; they have grown within the group as a practical adaptation to conditions of life which they could not change. This was essential if they were to survive.

If we examine more closely the structure of the early Negro family as represented in the situation studied, we find a distinct difference in the rôle of the mother. She has vastly greater authority in the Negro family than in the more familiar American family. This difference traces back directly to the values established around her rôle under slavery, when the father had no authority and exercised no control, since the woman belonged to the master and not to the husband. The authority of the Negro mother was reinforced by her relation with the white group, where she supported the "black mammy" tradition which survives feebly even today.

In the economic organization of the families of the Negro group studied, the earning power of the woman has been only slightly less than that of the man. This has given her an important measure of independence. Her prestige and importance has been further enhanced as a result of her advantage in dealing with the master class. Traditionally, she could ask greater favors, draw into the family small but constant sustenance, and in crises involving race tensions was always able to handle the situation better. The appearance of a male member of the group, except under circumstances of complete self-defeating humility, would often provoke punishment for impudence. These factors, among others, combined to give to the Negro woman in these early families a unique status, and this dominance is reflected today in many situations which the uninitiated fail to understand.

We may take for further illustration the familiar problems of illegitimacy and desertion, which show up in the urban setting. In the basic rural pattern, under the old plantation economy of slavery, these are not problems so much as they are phases of adjustment. They are not symptoms of disorganization as much as they are an organization of life for efficient functioning under exacting conditions.

Children born without legal sanctions, it was noted in the study, might be of several types, and these offspring cannot wisely be grouped together under the single classification of "illegitimate." Children of common-law relationships are not illegitimate from the point of view of the community or from the point of view of objective standards of stability and loyalty. Many common-law unions are as stable as the legally sanctioned ones; they sometimes hold together for twenty or thirty years, or until death removes one of the parties. Also there are competent, self-sufficient unmarried women who not only desire children but need them as later aids in the struggle for survival when their strength begins to wane. They want neither the restriction of a formal marriage contract nor the constant association with a husband.

There are, however, types of illegitimacy which are severely condemned by the community, such as the illegitimacy resulting from the deliberate philandering of young men who "make foolments" with young girls. Children falling under these categories may be placed with the parents of the mother or father or with an uncle, sister, or grandmother, as circumstance directs. They are accepted easily into the families and eventually are almost undistinguishable from any of the other children.

The practice of separation and divorce offers another example of group adaptation. In about a third of the families studied in the survey the man and woman were in their first association. Although the amount of remarriage is great, the number of divorces is extremely small. Voluntary and mutually desirable separation rarely ends in divorce. Divorce is one of the legal formalities introduced from the outside. Divorce is not essential to the functioning of the group life, since separation involves no serious problem of the care of children or the abandonment of helpless females. The courts, when such would normally be appealed to, are expensive and extrinsic to the social life; and, since the only contact with them is through officers of the law, who are more to be feared than trusted, such alien agencies are avoided. The meaning of divorce, in the sense in which it is usually employed, is thus considerably confounded.

Ownership of house or farm, and migration and education, are all indications that families are making new contacts and having dealings with other than their own intimate groups. Home ownership, for example, imposes a check upon adoption of children and upon the irregular organization of family groups. At this point, property and inheritance rights are involved, as are also stable credit and other business relations. Family traditions take on new meaning and are fostered. In other words, these are evidences that the families are acquiring, however imperfectly, new standards.

In communities characterized by home ownership, the educational level is higher and school facilities superior to those in old plantation tenant areas. Education has no place in this archaic culture, and often is more disturbing than helpful. Literacy and its tools are requisites of the owners and managers and their use by a tenant frequently leads to personal disaster.

When Negro families with the experience of slavery and social backwardness in their history are viewed in such a perspective, it is possible to avoid many of the harsh and irrelevant judgments so readily made. The situation of the

Negro migrant to the city has been, in fact, similar to that of the immigrant who, though a normal individual at home, makes many mistakes and is seriously misjudged in his new American setting. Without viewing these groups sympathetically, it is impossible to judge of their real capacity for citizenship.

The Negro family, usually as a result of economic forces, has experienced a variety of new conditions that have compelled readjustment in family habits. The result of this effort to readjust has very often been maladjustment. The most disturbing of these forces of change have been the adjustment of the rural Negro family to the urban environment, the introduction of machinery in agriculture, and, more recently, the depression, with its manifold problems. It may appear strange to discuss the Negro family from the point of view of the isolated rural Negro. This type of family is used simply as an example out of a frequently recurring situation in which there is so little participation in the social life of the community at large that the advancing standards are not adequately carried over. As a result, those who are cut off from this exchange devise a life of their own, which is essentially crude because of the meager materials with which they have to work. The same conditions hold whether the group is isolated by distance in the country or by the segregated areas of the towns.

There are, for example, a great many separations among Negro families in the towns. A moral judgment on this is prompt. But the provocation to separation may vary within wide limits. The economic system may not and often does not permit for the Negro male the same freedom of family control recognized within the white family. Women's work, even in the towns and cities, is more regulated, and a male may very often be an unwilling dependent. The male head of a family is at a disadvantage in exerting authority in a situation in which the dominant society takes a pride in his humiliation. When the courts condone irregularities among Negroes as racial and unmoral, the usefulness of the institution of the courts and the law as an instrument of control is lost. Where there are no channels of communication and social education, from what sources are the advanced standards expected to come? It is at this point that the settlements maintained by various religious organizations have found an important mission. The function that they serve, whatever they may call it, is that of relating these families securely to the best standards of life. It is this function that gives such high importance to the work with children.

The movement of Negro families from the country to cities of the South and North was accompanied by striking difficulties, some of them due to imperfect adoption of the city ways and to the persistence of old habits in a new environment. Other difficulties have been due to the situation which may be described as swinging free from the controls which regulated conduct in the old setting. This is essentially a phase of the process of moving from one set of standards to another. This necessity for "living in two worlds" can conceivably account for a great deal of the behavior of Negroes regarded as peculiar. It explains the so-called "bad nigger" and other types whose very strangeness and lack of adjustment make trouble for them. Modes of behavior which were once approved under formal social standards can take on quite a different character and become definitely anti-social in the light of new standards. Since notions of respectability rest so largely upon the social customs which have grown up with the group as a result of adaptation to its early social patterns, it is not difficult to understand why the desertion and separation rates are so high among Negro families. It is possible to understand the high illegitimacy rate which, for the United States as a whole in 1932, was 157.5 for every 1,000 Negro births as compared with 20.7 for every 1,000 births among the white population.

Wherever there is exposure to the approved American standards, and an opportunity for effective participation in general social life, change results. This can be observed within rural areas themselves where schools are introduced, literacy is increased, and new standards of health and social welfare are brought in. It can be observed likewise in the cities among the large numbers of Negroes who never shared this particular type of origin, or who are farther removed from it, and whose level of culture, as a result, is no different from that of their white neighbors.

CHAPTER FOUR

THE EDUCATION OF THE NEGRO

NEGRO education has been the focus of conflict-
ing theories and policies from the very beginning
of public education in America. Although it was
generally maintained by defenders of the institution of slavery
that Negroes were incapable of learning, virtually every slave
state passed stringent laws forbidding their education. The
punishment for instructing Negroes was a fine, or imprison-
ment for the offender, or both, and for the slave or free
Negro illegally receiving any such instruction, a public whip-
ping.

As in the case of the strict laws against manumission, however, there were violations and evasions by individuals whose
humanitarian impulses overcame their respect for such
measures. Some slaves and free Negroes received secret instruction and passed this meager learning on to others. Many
white children, in their innocence of the purpose of such a
ban, taught family slaves the alphabet as they would a children's game. Thus, when freedom came to the Negroes there
were some who could read and write, and a few who had

acquired by their own effort more education than the average white person.

The ban on Negro instruction, however, and the generally low state of public education before the middle of the nineteenth century, had the effect of keeping the illiteracy rate extremely high. Although there were fewer anti-education laws in the North, public sentiment and poverty served to accomplish practically the same end for the Negroes. It is estimated that between ninety-five and ninety-seven per cent of the Negroes were illiterate when they began their freedom.

In 1866 a few Southern cities but not a single Southern state had a system of free public schools.[1] The greatest hindrance to popular education was the race problem, because of the fear of mixed schools and because of the heavy burden of separate schools. Several years later, the strength of the growing Populist element again made common education an issue, as over against the aristocratic tradition which had prevailed. When, for example, it appeared that the only permanent method by which Negro suffrage could be restricted was through an educational qualification for voting, the race issue became a spur to the extension of public schools. In this manner the Negro helped the sentiment for public education but did not benefit greatly from it himself.

The most important aid to Negro education during this early period came through the Freedmen's Bureau, established

[1] "Some Phases of Educational History in the South Since 1865," by William K. Boyd, in *Studies in Southern History and Politics*, Columbia University Press, New York, 1914, p. 26.

by an act of Congress in 1865, and the missionary efforts of religious and other benevolent agencies. The first school for freedmen was opened on September 17, 1861, by the American Missionary Association at Fortress Monroe, in Virginia. A Negro woman, Mary S. Peake, was the teacher. It was the nucleus for Hampton Institute, and began the movement for the general education of Negroes in the South.

According to reports of the Freedmen's Bureau, during the first five years after the war, 4,239 schools were set up, with 9,307 teachers who were giving instruction to 247,333 pupils. The Negroes themselves raised enough funds to keep going 1,324 small schools and to purchase 592 buildings. During the intense political confusion of the period of Reconstruction, some public schools were established for Negro and white children by the Southern states. The school issue became entangled in the political conflict. In the end, however, the principle of common free schools for whites and Negroes was adopted, but Negro political participation was effectually eliminated.

The unexpectedly large numbers of white children requiring free public instruction, the poverty of the section, and the necessity for curtailing costs presented the temptation to experiment with the distribution of funds between white and Negro children. Thus began the inequalities in state expenditures which reached extreme lengths in some states and which continue to the present.[1] The "expedient" came about

[1] Horace Mann Bond, *The Education of the Negro in the American Social Order*, Prentice-Hall, New York, 1934, p. 115.

in this way. In many of the states with separate school systems, there are counties in which the Negro population is large, sometimes larger than the white. By reducing the amount per capita for Negro children, it was found that educational funds allotted to counties by the state, on the basis of the child population, could be made to yield a larger amount for white children. Thus, the greater the Negro population, the more funds there were that could be made available for white children.

The inequality, begun as an expedient, has been continued as a principle and has been given various justifications. It is explained that Negroes do not pay as much taxes and thus should not get as much of the educational fund. Again, it has been argued that the Negro child does not need as much education as the white child because there is less requirement for it in the work to which he is restricted. The curtailment of the Negro budget has resulted naturally in fewer schools for Negro children and thus fewer educable children in school, shorter school terms, lower salaries for Negro teachers, less equipment and general service. Under these circumstances it is no more than would be expected that the quality of education should be inferior, that these children should be greatly retarded, and that they should leave school before completing the fifth or sixth grade. It has been estimated that on the basis of the short school terms and the inadequate personnel, it would require in some areas seventeen years for the Negro child to complete the grammar grades.

Negro education received its most vital aid in the early

period from the missionary organizations which sent out hundreds of devoted workers. This was unquestionably one of the most valuable contributions to the adjustment to the new responsibilities of citizenship. Through these religious missionaries they got their first full exposure to American culture and the first real knowledge of what was expected of them in their new status. Those of the missionaries who came from the North resigned themselves to the social ostracism and at times the abuse which met their enterprise. They brought to the freedman an extraordinary background of education and an example of Christian devotion.

The missionary enterprise was, perhaps, the greatest single factor in making possible the complex adjustment of the changing Negro to his changing social environment. Missions kept elementary education active until the states could free themselves sufficiently to assume the support of public institutions. As the states took over the elementary schools the attention of the missionaries shifted to the secondary schools and later to the colleges, where they concerned themselves with preparing competent Negro teachers for the great masses requiring instruction.

The Negroes were eager for education and there has been a constant pressure of numbers on available facilities. In view of the difficulties imposed, the decline of illiteracy has been nothing less than phenomenal. Between 1865 and 1910 the rate dropped from 95 per cent to 30.4 per cent, and has continued to decline to the present. In 1930 the rate had reached 16.3 per cent.

A Preface to Racial Understanding

THE PRESENT EDUCATIONAL SITUATION

The assumption of responsibility for public education of Negroes has increased in the states with separate school systems, and appropriations for education have accordingly increased. The best comparative summary of present educational costs is provided in a pamphlet recently published by Fred McCuistion, agent for the Southern Association of Colleges and Secondary Schools. This summary indicates that at present the Negro child receives 37 per cent of the amount to which he is entitled on the basis of an equal distribution of public funds.

SUMMARY OF EXPENDITURES IN COLORED SCHOOLS [1]

State	Total Expended on Negro Schools	Additional Amount on Equal Basis	Percentage of Equal Expenditures Received by Negroes
Alabama	$ 1,964,524	$ 3,515,946	36
Arkansas	1,443,306	2,141,680	40
Florida	1,302,623	2,881,090	31
Georgia	1,667,884	4,273,514	28
Louisiana	2,542,213	5,028,664	33
Maryland	2,230,857	912,928	71
Mississippi	1,583,541	6,015,099	21
North Carolina	4,086,792	4,409,217	48
Oklahoma	1,657,544	432,544	79
South Carolina	1,718,854	6,056,927	22
Texas	3,263,821	4,020,443	45
Total	$23,461,959	$39,688,052	37

[1] Adapted from a table in "Financing Schools in the South," by Fred McCuistion, Julius Rosenwald Fund, Chicago, p. 18.

The Education of the Negro

If any satisfaction is to be drawn from these figures it is from the fact that the states with separate school systems spent $23,461,959 in 1930 for Negro education. But it is noted that the South is less able than other sections, financially, to support the cost of education. The average per capita wealth in the South is $1,785, as compared with $3,609 for the states outside the South. To make matters more serious, the South has assumed the obligation of supporting two separate school systems. In the end, both systems suffer. The average expenditure for each pupil for education in the nation at large is $99. For white children in the South it is $44.31 and for Negro children $12.57, or about a fourth of the amount expended on white children in the South and one-eighth of the amount expended on the average for children in the country as a whole.

The disproportion in expenditures varies by states. In Mississippi the amount spent annually for each white child is $45.34 and for each Negro child, $5.45. It is estimated that the Negro child in the deep South has about one-fifteenth of the educational opportunity of the average American child. Because it has a bearing upon the type of Negro teacher available for the Negro child and the income of Negroes generally, it should be mentioned that the average annual salary of white teachers in 1930 was $901 and of Negro teachers, $423. Thus for the same or, in some instances, an even greater volume of work, the Negro teacher receives somewhat less than 47 per cent of the salary of the white teacher.

71

A Preface to Racial Understanding

The gross inadequacy of Negro elementary education has prompted private philanthropy to aid it. The most conspicuous contribution in this connection has been the Rosenwald Schools. Beginning his assistance quietly as an experiment in education, Mr. Julius Rosenwald in 1911 made a provisional gift of funds for the erection of rural school buildings for Negroes in Alabama. This was done at the suggestion of Booker T. Washington. It was stipulated that the donor would provide a proportion of a total sum raised by the state taxing bodies and by private Negro and white contributions. This was, perhaps, one of the most profitable single investments made in Negro education. When this program closed in 1932, there were 5,357 Rosenwald schools with a capacity of 663,615 children. The total cost had been around $28,000,000, and of this amount Mr. Rosenwald had contributed about 15.4 per cent, the Negroes 16.6 per cent and the tax funds 64 per cent. The great value had been in setting a higher standard in rural education and stimulating the states to live up to it. In the end elementary education in the South profited generally.

Antedating the Rosenwald Fund was the Peabody Fund, which, as early as 1880, began to concern itself with the training of teachers in the South. It aided both white and Negro institutions, and was not dissolved until 1914. The Slater Fund aimed to direct itself to the higher education of Negroes, but at the time of its beginning in 1882 Negro higher education was at the high school level. It has contributed to the lifting of the level of this advanced training. The fund established by Miss Anna T. Jeanes, a Philadelphia Quaker, is responsible for the invaluable "Jeanes teachers," demonstration agents for rural schools, who are the medium through which educational standards are communicated to the isolated rural teachers, and the educational world, in turn, is kept aware of the isolated rural child. Both the Slater and the Jeanes funds were effectively administered by Dr. James Harvey Dillard of Charlottesville, Virginia, over a number of years until his retirement a few years ago, when he was succeeded by Dr. Arthur T. Wright.

But for the General Education Board, established in 1903, it is probable that the higher education of Negroes would have been greatly retarded, to the detriment of the program of providing a competent Negro teaching force for the elementary and secondary schools. Over $20,000,000 have been contributed to Negro education by this board. The Phelps-Stokes Fund, under the direction of Dr. Thomas Jesse Jones, has concerned itself with Negro education in both America and Africa.

The church boards have been the most consistent supporters of Negro education on the secondary and college level.[1] Practically all of the Negro private colleges are supported by one or the other of these boards. Nine such agencies contribute annually over $1,700,000 to Negro education. They hold nearly $10,000,000 in permanent funds for Negro educa-

[1] See *Negro Year Book* for 1931-32, pp. 211-13.

tion, and the school plants which they support are at present valued at more than $20,000,000.

NEGRO EDUCATION IN THE NORTH

The problems of Negro elementary education are not limited to the states having separate schools. In the Northern states, Negro and white children have attended the same schools. Following the migration of large numbers of Negroes from the poorer schools of the South to the Northern centers there was noted an increasing disposition to group them separately. Some of the school authorities complained that the serious retardation of the Southern children constituted sufficient warrant for separate treatment. However, as numbers of studies have shown, the retardation was, in a large measure, gradually overcome.

The most considerable factor in educational segregation has been residential segregation. The educational policy now varies widely between cities. Philadelphia, Trenton, and Indianapolis are examples of cities in which there are separate schools and in which the Negro schools have Negro principals. In New York City no race distinction is made, but as a result of the high residential concentration the effect is about the same. However, Negroes may attend any school in the city, and Negro teachers are not restricted to schools with the largest Negro membership but may teach in any in which a vacancy occurs. In Cincinnati, there are both mixed and separate schools.

There has been much discussion around the relative edu-

74

cational values for Negro children of the two types of schools. On the one hand, it is urged that the mixed school insures equal facilities and standards, and an opportunity for white and Negro pupils to meet normally. On the other hand, it is insisted that the increased opportunity for Negro teachers, the more intimate interest of these teachers in Negro pupils, and the avoidance of racial friction constitute a superior advantage. With increased numbers of Negroes in the Northern cities the tendency to segregation increases, and this tendency is viewed with apprehension by many Negroes. Recent studies of Negro educational achievement indicate that Negro children in Northern schools rank far above the Negro children in Southern schools and show no important difference in educational achievement from white pupils.

INDUSTRIAL EDUCATION

Industrial education for Negroes was advocated as early as 1828 when Martin R. Delany, one of the foremost Negroes of the period, expressed the view that "we should first be mechanics and common tradesmen, and professions as a matter of course would grow out of the wealth made thereby." Twenty-five years later Frederick Douglass expressed a similar opinion when he commented to Harriet Beecher Stowe that Negroes needed "more to learn how to make a good living than to learn Latin and Greek." The early industrial schools were designed to supply a need for apprenticeship opportunities. Naturally the industrial schools were sporadic and of little moment until the extensive education program was undertaken for freedmen following the Civil War.

Shortly after the outbreak of the Civil War, President Lincoln signed the Morrill Act, July 2, 1862, and thereby made possible the establishment of colleges of agricultural and mechanical arts throughout the United States. This proposed general industrial education did not get under way until the end of the war, and even then these state schools made no special provision for Negroes.

Under the Reconstruction government, Negro schools were included in the educational program. The basis was laid for support of agricultural and mechanical schools through federal aid. Further legislation for the encouragement of this type of education was passed in 1890. Public encouragement was given in the granting of funds to these schools, but through private interest the idea of training for Negroes was fostered and influenced most.

In 1867 the American Missionary Association adopted the urgent suggestion of General Samuel C. Armstrong that a normal school be established. The following year General Armstrong was called upon to head the school which became known as Hampton Normal and Agricultural Institute, a school destined to be a most potent force in the development of industrial education for Negroes. He introduced a type of training he had observed to be of value in his native Hawaii. There the Hilo Boarding and Manual Labor School gave a type of training which in its adoption by Armstrong was to be known in Negro education as the "Hampton idea."

The Education of the Negro

Instead of following the course of the other missionary schools of the period he concentrated on simple English instruction and training in industrial pursuits. In 1870 Hampton Institute, along with a private theological school in Virginia, qualified for federal aid under the Morrill Act and in 1872, though remaining a private school, became the land-grant college for Negroes in Virginia. It was thus receiving special federal aid almost a score of years before the establishment of the Negro land-grant colleges in the states maintaining separate school systems.

In 1875 the person destined to become the greatest champion of industrial education for Negroes was graduated from Hampton Institute. Six years later Booker T. Washington became principal of Tuskegee Institute and the program outlined for that institution by him and executed with his powerful technique was to make it of greater importance than Hampton in promoting industrial training on a large scale. The enunciation of Mr. Washington's philosophy in his famous speech, delivered at the Atlanta Exposition in 1895, led to the battle for industrial education between himself and his critics which lasted until his death in 1915.

The popularity of industrial and technical education grew with the development and expansion of Tuskegee Institute. The agricultural and mechanical colleges for Negroes in the South took over in varying degrees the Tuskegee program of instruction. These institutions were called on to prepare teachers for the common schools in their respective states and in the course of their development some tended to neglect

77

the industrial phase of their work. This was encouraged through the difficulty with which equipment was procured for full training in the crafts and skills. The cost of industrial education, requiring shops, tools, and machinery, was much greater than that of classroom instruction, and in many instances most earnest advocates of the Tuskegee idea found themselves handicapped by lack of facilities. However, valiant attempts were made to carry on this type of work and in 1916 Dr. Thomas Jesse Jones listed sixty-one public and private institutions offering some industrial training.

The schools of higher learning pointed the way for secondary education, and with the preparation of teachers in the schools of higher grade, industrial training was introduced into the high schools. The industrial training was not of a very high grade in the public schools because of the lack of facilities for instruction. The city schools made the first attempts at incorporating industrial instruction into the curriculum and it was not until 1911-12 that any noteworthy progress was made in introducing it into rural schools. In that school year the first county training schools were established with aid from the Jeanes and Slater funds. There has been a steady increase in the number of these institutions since that time. Industrial training was further encouraged by the passage of the Smith-Hughes Act in 1917. This legislation gave federal aid in the payment of salaries of agricultural, mechanical arts, and some economics instructors in the common schools.

Industrial and technical training for Negroes has lagged

behind that of the country at large. Two factors have influenced this. One was the opposition of a large element of Negroes at a period of its development and the other was the hesitancy of school systems to make proper expenditures to provide for it in Negro schools. In the present period, when most city school systems boast at least one public technical high school of the finest type, the work in Negro schools is as a rule scarcely more than crude instruction in obsolete crafts and skills which are useless in a period of machine production. With the growth of technical education through all levels of instruction in the school system, facilities for Negro education along classic lines have improved and the technical training has become less immediately useful, although there is undoubted value in the general technical discipline provided.

THE NEGRO COLLEGE

The first Negro schools which took the name of colleges were really elementary and secondary schools. Gradually the standards have been raised as the educational acquirements of the Negro population have increased. The aim of the first schools was to develop teachers and ministers in answer to an insistent demand for leadership. In spite of the uneven character of the schools much of the first objective was accomplished.

The present outstanding Negro colleges owe their existence in large part to the continued support of the various church organizations through their missionary and education boards. All these schools, with the exception of the state institutions and those founded by Negro denominations, began with white teachers, many of whom continue on the faculties of the Negro colleges today, even in notable instances in which a Negro has been elected to the presidency.

The Methodist Episcopal Church created the now famed Freedman's Aid Society. The American Missionary Association, founded in 1846 "for the propagation of free Christianity from which the sins of caste, polygamy, slaveholding, and the like shall be excluded," was, as indicated earlier, the first to send missionaries for the education of Negroes after their emancipation. They originally represented the Congregationalists, the Presbyterians, and the Reformed Dutch and Associate Reformed churches. Such institutions as Fisk University in Nashville, Tennessee; Atlanta University in Georgia; Straight College in New Orleans, now merged into the new Dillard University; Hampton Institute; and Berea College in Kentucky, now by state law an exclusively white school, are an outgrowth of their early efforts.

The American Baptist Home Mission Society, active since the emancipation of the slaves, has operated twenty-six Negro schools in thirteen states. Among these are Virginia Union University in Richmond; Morehouse College and Spelman College in Atlanta, Georgia, both now merged with Atlanta University; and Shaw University in Raleigh, North Carolina. The Board of Education of the Methodist Episcopal Church is responsible for another group of schools, among which are Bennett College in Greensboro, North Carolina; Wiley College in Marshall, Texas; Clark University in Atlanta, Georgia; and Gammon Theological Seminary, also in Atlanta. Paine College, in Augusta, Georgia, is maintained cooperatively by the Methodist Episcopal Church, South, and the Colored Methodist Episcopal Church. The Board of National Missions of the Presbyterian Church in the United States of America has founded several schools, the most important of which is Johnson C. Smith University in Charlotte, North Carolina.

One of the most drastic and yet helpful crises in Negro higher education was that precipitated by the study of Negro colleges by Dr. Thomas Jesse Jones in 1916 for the Department of the Interior. He was bluntly honest in his appraisals of these colleges against the general standard of American higher education. The report condemned inefficient institutions and caused the elimination of many of them, but an important result was the inauguration of a period of higher educational standards. Today there are eighteen or twenty Negro colleges with full accreditation under the strictest standards of American education. Many others are not far behind and are striving to reach these standards. In 1921 there were about 5,000 Negro college students enrolled in institutions with recognized collegiate departments. This number had increased in 1932 to 22,609 and in 1935 to 25,000.

STATE-CONTROLLED COLLEGES

The most encouraging sign in Negro education is the increasing assumption of responsibility for higher education by the states. The federal government in 1890 entered seriously the field of Negro higher education, under the new Morrill Act, with grants-in-aid for Negro state institutions. In the separate-school states, the act of 1890 insisted that there should be no discrimination against Negroes, and this meant separate Negro colleges for agricultural and mechanical instruction. It became evident early that these Negro institutions would have to remedy some of the deficiencies of the elementary schools. At first all of the "colleges" were either normal schools or industrial and agricultural institutions. Gradually there developed liberal arts departments in the institutions which, though referred to as colleges and universities, had been doing most of their work on the high school level. In 1916 only 12 students of college grade were enrolled in the 17 land-grant colleges; in 1930 there were 5,676 college students in a total enrolment of 17,765. In 1933, from a tabulation made by President John W. Davis of the West Virginia Collegiate Institute, the 17 Negro state land-grant colleges were receiving a total of $9,339,610, about half of which came from federal funds and half from the states.

THE NEGRO COLLEGE GRADUATE

Since John Russwurm received his bachelor of arts degree from Bowdoin in 1826, there have been 39,000 Negro college and professional graduates. These graduates did not begin to appear in any important numbers until 1890. In 1900 there had been only about 2,331 known graduates of these institutions. Between 1914 and 1934 there were 28,083 who received degrees, 18.8 per cent of these from Northern institutions and 81.2 per cent from Negro colleges chiefly in the South. There were as many graduates during the eight year period 1924-1932 as there had been over the preceding ninety-eight years, 1826-1924.

These graduates represent, in the range of their occupations, some two hundred or more skills, but the majority are concentrated in the six fields: teaching, medicine, the ministry, law, social and religious work, business.

Most of these graduates are located in the South at present, but the border states have the largest proportion of college graduates in relation to the size of the Negro population. In 1933 the twelve most southern states had 11.9 graduates for every 10,000 Negroes, the Northern states 21.8, the Western states 23.1 and the border states 36.5.[1]

The demand for trained persons in the familiar fields has been so great in the past that it has been possible for many to enter upon them with a fair measure of success, even though they were without any special ability for the professions. Competition has not been extremely keen, the schools in which many of them were prepared were not up to the standard of a good college, the requirements of their Negro clientele were not especially high, and the requirements of the certifying authorities even less exacting. With the increasing number of these graduates, and with the increased efficiency of the schools, there is appearing, perhaps for the first time,

[1] Charles S. Johnson, *The Negro College Graduate*. University of North Carolina Press, Chapel Hill, 1936.

a test of fitness which will eliminate many who are unfit for the professions which they choose now so largely on the basis of the positions most likely to be open rather than because of interest or aptitude. Such a situation will eventually compel experimentation in new fields where racial prejudice is least likely to interfere seriously with careers. But such inclination to experimentation in or broadening of the occupational range is not yet conspicuously in evidence either in the high schools or in the colleges.

THE FUTURE OF NEGRO EDUCATION

There is considerable controversy at present over the question of the education of Negroes. Twenty years ago there was a similar controversy over the relative merits of vocational and classical education. Dr. W. E. B. DuBois, thirty years ago, strongly advocated the cause of higher education against the insistence of Booker T. Washington that industrial education was the first immediate need. In reviewing his position on this question recently, Dr. DuBois commented that this controversy was between two opposing schools of thought. On the one hand there were those who contended that the economic adaptation of the Negro to the South must, in education, be subordinated to the great necessity of teaching a way of life and imparting a culture. This was primarily an appeal for leadership. On the other hand, the practical-minded men of the South argued that this was an individual and business age. No rising group of peasants could begin at the top. If they were to survive, their children must be taught the dignity of the work which the great masses of the Negroes would undoubtedly have to do for many years to come.

Today that issue is yet unsettled, although we have lost much of the original purpose of the vocational schools in the desire to make more colleges. Technical education has come into vogue and its cost, whether or not warranted in result, is sufficiently prohibitive to local administrations to prompt them to encourage for Negroes the classical fields of study which had been at first denied them. These require no elaborate machinery and equipment.

The new controversy is an amusingly specious one: whether there should be such a thing as specifically Negro education, or whether Negroes should be given the same kind of education as all other Americans.

There are as many types of educational institutions in America as there are definitions of education. An underlying assumption, however, of most of these definitions, as well as institutions, is that we are educating or being educated with reference to fixed conditions. Actually, the essence of these conditions is change itself, a fact which gives a new coloring to all our educational preparation. It makes imperative the linking of study with life, and life is in constant change. Moreover, objectives of the many types of educational practice in America are determined by conceptions of these conditions and by the actual circumstances of the mass of individuals who are the concern of the institution.

Simple common sense seems to indicate that there are

special stresses and even philosophies to which Negroes would do well to give attention, as a measure of survival in the new society.

There is an undeniable lag in Negro status, partly due to a handicapping social environment and partly due to Negroes themselves. It must be overcome if Negroes are to survive in the present competitive society. There may be a romantic niche for the stereotyped temperament of the Negro, his wit and humor, his emotional resistance to the machine age, but so long as he must win his bread in this age in competition with hands and minds geared to this new phase of the economic revolution, he must at least be equally equipped; and if he is to succeed he must be better equipped and recognize the necessity for it.

The ineffectiveness of many of the vocational schools has been due largely to the attempt to pass along specific skills. Dr. Abraham Flexner has drawn a nice distinction between education and training. A man or youth may be trained to make a broom or a pair of shoes or a box without being educated in mechanics or woodcraft or the fabrication of fibers. It is futile to provide a training in an archaic trade merely because it is simple. It is likewise futile to attempt to impart a specific skill for the intensely specialized and rapidly changing process of modern industry. What seems to be required is the development in Negro youth of general mechanical techniques with the thoroughness that the liberal arts colleges employ, in theory at least, in developing an undifferentiated cultural competence. And, as is expected of a liberal arts education, this technique may be transferred and applied to the specific task demanding it.

This education, this development of a technique, a sense for accuracy, precision, craftsmanship and creative art, should begin even earlier than the vocational school; it should begin in the grades, and this is a challenge to the new education.

CHAPTER FIVE

THE CONTRIBUTION OF THE NEGRO
TO AMERICAN CIVILIZATION

ALL too frequently in estimates of our own national greatness we overlook the contributions of other groups at earlier stages of this greatness—contributions without which there would have been a very different course of history. From ancient China came gunpowder and the art of printing, two of the most powerful instruments of Western civilization. From ancient India came symbols of number, the decimal system, algebra and trigonometry. From the Phœnicians came the alphabet. From the Semites came the Christian religion. From Africa came the art of iron smelting. From the Arabs came chemistry. The list could be extended indefinitely, but this is perhaps enough to suggest the mutal obligation of the peoples of the world to one another for what each enjoys as his own civilization.

The nature of these contributions varies according to the rôle played by the separate groups in the broad plan of civilization. No one would think today of disparaging the talents of women because they have not been the world's great explorers or fighters or even artists and scholars, although, strange to say, such observations have been made in the past and given "scientific" support. It is only recently that women have escaped from the grip of custom which has restricted the range of their participation in what has been regarded as a man's world. They have, nevertheless, made a vital contribution to the progress of civilization, although their achievements have largely been anonymous.

The Negro group presents a situation analogous to that of women. Their most important contributions to American civilization have too often been obscured because, by the very nature of these contributions, they have lacked the element of high drama, of quixotic characters; because they have been, for the most part, made anonymously.

THE GIFT OF LABOR

The first and most vital contribution of the Negro was the labor which cleared the forests, dug the mines, grew the staples which were the material foundation of the New World. The coming of the Negroes was dictated by the demand for labor and labor only. It was this labor that paved the way for the machine, for the full flowering of the industrial age, for big business—of which the slave traffic itself was the first. Negroes followed Columbus and the *conquistadores* and worked the mines in the first impetuous search for gold after the Indians had perished by the hundreds of thousands. The Negroes did not die, but out of their brawn new wealth was created.

A Preface to Racial Understanding

Their labor supported tobacco, the first staple crop of the New World. They alone could live in the miasmic swamps where rice, another staple, was grown. Black sugar-makers from Barbadoes supported the first successful cane refining experiments in Louisiana, and other workers manned the cane plantations. The world knows the story of cotton—how Negroes cultivated all of it at the time the South commanded the cotton market of the world. The great battles of the world were won not by the Cæsars who survived to write their memoirs but by the nameless soldiers who died to make possible these victories.

Not only was there this vital contribution of brawn; there was a surprising amount of skill, and even genius, in the Negroes' gift of labor. Historians note that Negroes early became the skilled artisans for the Virginia colony. In the census of Charleston, South Carolina, in 1850, they were noted in fifty-six different occupations. A Negro bootmaker made by hand the shoes in which President Monroe was inaugurated. Harriet Martineau, when she visited America, marveled at the exquisite patterns of the tiling in Thomas Jefferson's home, laid by his Negro artisan. Workers in hand-wrought iron marked a period in the architecture of old New Orleans with their delicately patterned iron porticos, trellises and galleries. The magnificent old mansions which remain today as symbols of the romantic Old South were built by these Negro artisans.

When the city of Washington was being planned by Major Pierre Charles L'Enfant, the reputation of the Negro astronomer and mathematician, Benjamin Banneker, was sufficiently established to prompt President George Washington to send for him, at the suggestion of Thomas Jefferson, and appoint him as one of the six commissioners. It is recorded that he performed an important part of the mathematical calculations of the survey and took part in the conferences with the other commissioners.

Much of the skill and genius of invention of these workers will remain unknown simply because no slave could obtain a patent in his own name. A classic test of this was made by Jefferson Davis himself, when he attempted to secure a patent for his slave, B. T. Montgomery, the father of the founder of the Negro colony of Mound Bayou, Mississippi. Occasionally the identity of a Negro invention could be established as, for example, in the cases of Henry Blair, a Maryland Negro, who invented a successful corn planter, and Norbert Rillieux, who invented a complicated vacuum pan, revolutionizing the then known method of refining sugar. A Negro named Matzelinger invented a machine for lasting shoes, thereby removing bootmaking from the handicrafts to the factory and reducing the cost of manufacture by fifty per cent. The patent was purchased by the United States Machinery Company. In the United States Patent Office a few years ago, a check-up revealed that there were over fifteen hundred inventions made by Negroes, and that this was only a partial list. In the wide field of modern science there have been as yet few notable Negro contributions, because as a race they have not been long enough exposed to this intricate current of development. One need only mention the name of Ernest Just and his international reputation as a biologist, to augur the future of the Negro in this field. But as this civilization has taught the Negroes *things,* Negroes in turn have taught this civilization *feelings.* Their religious expression best attests this.

It is customary in referring to the Negro's contribution to American civilization to attempt to isolate unique culture traits brought from Africa. This is difficult because from the very nature of their Americanization few of these traits could survive. Despite a cultural detachment more complete than that experienced by any other group coming to America, there has undoubtedly been persistence of intangible elements of the native culture. But, what is more important, there has been the creation in a new and alien setting of powerful motifs in music, rhythm, folklore, and the dance.

THE GIFT OF MUSIC

Perhaps the best known and most widely recognized of the Negro's gifts to America is his music. The folk songs have been of varied types and character. Without doubt the most important, and at the same time the most appealing, of these have been the religious songs. The best of them —the spirituals—were born in the slave era when, as one commentator puts it, "heartstrings were taut." In addition to the spirituals there are work songs, social songs, "blues," ballads and "mellows."

Spirituals. The spirituals, which evolved in the American setting, have been regarded as the "only distinctively Ameri-

The Contribution of the Negro

can folk music." At least the great European composer,
Dvořák, believed so, and his judgment has been confirmed
by numerous other critics. It is interesting to note that the
African pattern of music is apparently not so closely related
to American Negro spirituals as is the latter to the early
American religious hymns. Whether the basis of the spirituals
was African music or the religious hymns heard in America,
it is certain that a new and distinct musical product is the
result.

These spirituals are scarcely matched by any other group
of songs in the simple beauty of their melody or in the powerful imagery of their lines. The stories of the Bible had a
mighty appeal to the rich imagination of the slaves. From the
Christian religion itself they drew comfort and hope enough
to sustain their bodies and their spirits through long dark
years. There is in the music such childlike faith, such an
absoluteness of reliance upon the promise of religion, such
a warmly human conception of Divinity, that the music
embodying this religion transcends the very special circumstances of its creation and becomes a medium for expressing
the sorrows and joys and hopes of men generally. The mere
titles of a few of these tell their own story: "Nobody Knows
de Trouble I See"; "Steal Away to Jesus"; "Go Down,
Moses"; "My Lord, What a Morning!"; "Swing Low, Sweet
Chariot"; "Sometimes I Feel Like a Motherless Child"; "Oh,
Stand the Storm, It Won't Be Long; We'll Anchor By and
By"; "Deep River, My Home Is Over Jordan"; "I Want to
Be Ready to Walk in Jerusalem Jus' Like John"; "I Couldn't

Hear Nobody Pray"; "Done Made My Vow to de Lord"; "Can't You Live Humble?"; "God Is a God."

The music must be heard to be appreciated, and most Americans are now familiar with it. However, the words themselves are charged with such emotional intensity and such stark imagery as to give them unmistakable meaning, even through the folk speech. When Negroes sing "Death's Gwineter Lay His Cold Icy Hands on Me," or "Jesus Gonna Make Up My Dying Bed," or "I Feel Like My Time Ain't Long," or "Don't You Let Nobody Turn You 'Round," they reveal a faith intimately involved with life. A comparison of the Negro themes with the biblical texts which inspired them shows how completely they made these passages their own:

"I will send him against an hypocritical nation" [*Isaiah* 10:6].
  Spiritual: "Hypercrite, Hypercrite, de Lawd Despise."
"Thou sawest that a stone was cut out without hands" [*Daniel* 2:34].
  Spiritual: "Daniel Saw de Stone."
"What are these which are arrayed in white robes? and whence came they?" [*Revelation* 7:13].
  Spiritual: "Who's dat comin' all dressed in white?
          Must be de chillun of de Israelite."

Undoubtedly there was some borrowing from the early hymns, but in the borrowing the folk Negro versions contribute a new quality. In his volume, *White Spirituals in the*

The Contribution of the Negro

Uplands, Professor George Pullen Jackson cites certain hymns out of which the Negroes made spirituals. One hymn reads:

> He gave his soul up to the stroke
> Without a murmuring word.

The Negro version reads simply:

> An' he never said a mumblin' word.

Another hymn verse reads:

> I have my bitter and my sweet
> As through this world I travel;
> I sometimes shout and sometimes weep
> Which makes my foes to marvel.

The Negro slave sang:

> Sometimes I'm up, sometimes I'm down,
> Sometimes I'm almost to de groun'.

These songs were first carried to the world by the Fisk Jubilee Singers who, in 1871, began a pilgrimage which made the spirituals famous throughout Europe and America. In his magnificent volume, *The Souls of Black Folk,* W. E. Burghardt DuBois calls them sorrow songs, and so well states a sentiment which has been time and again repeated that it seems fitting to quote him:

"Little of beauty has America given the world save the rude grandeur of God himself stamped on her bosom; the human spirit in this new world has expressed itself in vigor and ingenuity rather than in beauty. And so by fateful chance the Negro folksong—the rhythmic cry of the slave—stands today not simply as the sole American music, but as the most beautiful expression of human experience born this side of the seas. It has been neglected; it has been, and is, half despised, and above all it has been persistently mistaken and misunderstood; but notwithstanding, it still remains as the singular spiritual heritage of the nation and the greatest gift of the Negro people." [1]

Social Songs. Whereas melody is the dominant note of the spirituals, rhythm is the dominant note of other distinctively Negro music, some of which has become the foundation of American popular music. There is in African music, as Dr. George Herzog of Yale has pointed out, a development of rhythm so far beyond the European that successful recording of it has not yet been accomplished. While this rhythm is incidental to African music, it is dominant in the syncopation of the American music, and this has set the pattern for the modern popular music of America and Europe.

Back of jazz is the so-called "coon song," back of the "coon song" is the minstrel show, back of the minstrel show is the plantation melody, and back of the plantation melody is the spiritual. Stephen Foster attributes to these melodies the inspiration and even the structure of his sentimental ballads "My Old Kentucky Home," "Way Down Upon the Swanee River," and others—which the Americans today know better than they do the national anthem.

[1] W. E. Burghardt DuBois, *The Souls of Black Folk,* A. C. McClurg & Co., Chicago, 1903, p. 251.

The Contribution of the Negro

The extent of incorporation of these Negro cultural specializations in the American culture may be well illustrated in the case of jazz music. The origin of jazz music is the syncopation of the Negro. There has been much more weighty discussion of this type of American music than the subject would seem to warrant in some quarters. Gilbert Seldes has observed that jazz expresses "the complicated vigor of American life." Paul Whiteman calls it the "spirit of a new country" and asserts that it "catches up the underlying motif of a continent and period, molding it into a form which expresses the fundamental emotion of the people, the place and time, so authentically that it is immediately recognizable." Isaac Goldberg, a noted critic of music, asks seriously if jazz is a technique or a mood, and after calling it both, observes that the symphonic scherzo derives from a dance spirit that is not far removed in origin from the spirit of jazz. Copland thinks that the chief influence of jazz will be in the development of poly-rhythm, providing the American composer with an instrument he can operate and utilize. As much could be said of the music called the "blues." These are, in a way, personal lamentations of Negroes over constant misfortune, but they have, unfortunately, been taken over by the white world, commercialized, and greatly vulgarized.

THE GIFT OF FOLKLORE

Joel Chandler Harris is responsible for bringing formally to the attention of the world the Uncle Remus stories of Br'er Rabbit and other delightful characters with which Negro slaves had long entertained the children of the South. These stories have had a fascination for childhood unmatched by any other set of characters in American children's literature. Many of these trace back to Africa; others are modifications of themes borrowed from Europe; and still others are pure creation. Back of the real charm of the stories is the quite evident fact that a vivid imagination had been fostered in the Negroes by the cramping realities of their everyday life. It is interesting to note that these stories have animal characters who behave like humans but who retain at the same time their animal nature. Some of the stories suggest that the opportunity for social criticism by the slave was not wholly lost.

In addition to the animal stories and the rick folk philosophy which they embodied, there is a wealth of legend and tall tales providing high dramatization of incidents, great and trivial. Unhampered by conventional literature as a result of his illiteracy, the Negro has created new folk materials of unfailing beauty and human appeal. No one who has seen the play by Marc Connelly, *The Green Pastures,* which attempted to record a Negro folk interpretation of the Bible, could fail to catch fragments of an authentic religious fervor and a spirit of intimate fellowship with the Deity. No other medium than the Negro folk story could have sustained so daring a venture of the drama into the realm of the sacrosanct.

Traits developed by the Negro as a survival measure have, in time, become leavening for the white people. Notable among them are a rich sense of humor, a simple trusting religion, and a philosophy of life which has relieved their existence of much of its tense emptiness. That these are characteristic traits not only of the Negro but of his status is suggested in the fact that all three can be lost when Negroes become thoroughly Americanized.

THE GIFT OF HUMOR

The cheerfulness of the older Negroes is proverbial. Their simple but ready humor has provided an antidote for a grim and hard age. By this humor they aided their own survival, softened the rigors of the class lines forcibly imposed, provided entertainment, and taught a cold and melancholy world how to laugh at trouble. But there was more than this to their humor. It was a protective device. A humorous turn, a clumsily ambiguous phrase, an exaggerated gesture in deference to stereotypes about graveyards, ghosts, watermelons, razors, rampant flight from danger and like histrionics could win both tolerance and favors, when direct and manly dealings on any score would be interpreted as unbecoming insolence.

RELIGION

There has been much comment, both generous and deprecatory, concerning the religion of the early American Negro and of many of the contemporary Negroes as well. A common observation is that theirs is a sort of convulsive Christianity which expresses itself in noisy emotional outbursts accompanied by physical demonstrations of various sorts. It is true that this pattern of worship has been and still is associated with the Negro group of the past, but it is also true that the pattern was borrowed along with the doctrine from the old camp meetings of the early South. As late as thirty years ago shouting, jerking and convulsions were fairly common among rural and somewhat isolated whites, who merely carried on the camp meeting tradition after it had been generally discarded. Where the gospel is carried to native Africans in Africa by missionaries with different habits, no such demonstrations are characteristic.

It might be supposed that the cultural base of the transplanted African provided difficult soil for the development of the seed of Christianity. But the Bible was the sole literature of the slave, and the reading of it practically the sole end of such instruction as he received. The Christian religion itself, far from being an abstract theism suited only for an advanced civilization, was in principle and doctrine a religion which could be accepted at full value by the Negro. It taught humility in an age of aggressive, heedless pioneering and conquest. It exalted the lowly, disparaged the cold and needless accumulation of worldly goods at the cost of human suffering, glorified the despised who, acting on the inspiration of Christ, forgot their age-old enmities in the greater spiritual glory of tolerance and forgiveness. It taught the oneness of mankind, promised a rich reward in heaven for earthly suffering. It was a religion and a doctrine which the slave could take in deeply and fully. The eagerness to decipher these words from the sacred text, the strength of conviction regarding the eternal truth of these principles, are in themselves evidence of the power of appeal to the slaves who, having little on earth to hope for, fixed their hopes firmly on heaven.

It was observed rather generally that Christian instruction made Negroes better slaves and better workers. They complained less about their lot, found solace in their high hopes of heaven, forgave wrongs, and contented themselves with deferred rewards for a good life in the midst of disillusioning hardship. There is no greater testimony to the intimate influence of a gospel. If this was misunderstood, or ridiculed, or rationalized as the natural behavior of weaker minds it could scarcely be the fault either of Negro faith or of Christian doctrine. The genuine test of the solacing powers of the Christian religion was their life, and the greatest demonstration of faith and hope, to the point of serenity and physical increase, was provided by these Negroes. Whatever their present estimate of the value of faith, they did provide in the past the most convincing demonstration of the power of the spirit of Christianity to move the world. The gift of an unmatched example of loyalty and faith may be counted an important one in a troubled and unsettled world.

LITERATURE AND ART

The contributions of Negroes to the fields of letters and art give promise of a tremendous enrichment of both the literature and life of the whole people. Because this field is not so well known, it will, perhaps, be useful to review it briefly.

A Preface to Racial Understanding

Early Negro literature, like early American literature, is more interesting as history than as creative expression. Both were unnaturally influenced by literary patterns alien to their experience; both were damaged on the one hand by rather excessive claims to importance as literature, and on the other by ruthless, sometimes disdainful, comparisons with older literature and peoples. Both reflected, above all else, the violent currents of thought and life in the New World, and, with striking frequency, the very same currents from different planes.

A necessary distinction should be made between the writing which is Negro literature in the sense of expressing a group consciousness, and that writing on non-racial themes by men who merely happened to be Negroes. The not inconsiderable list of theological treatises by such Negroes as Lemuel Haynes, N. C. Cannon, William Catto, and Alexander Crummell, and even the verse of Jupiter Hammon, who antedates Phillis Wheatley, when construed broadly as literature, fall within this latter class and are roughly analogous to the theological writings of Jonathan Edwards, the Mathers, and the religious poetry of Wigglesworth. It would well repay the search to read some of the early theological literature of Negro writers.[1]

Phillis Wheatley, the slave poetess who published her first volume of verse in 1773 at the age of twenty, belonged to the colonial period in more than one sense. She came some years after Anne Bradstreet, the first American woman poet, with

[1] An interesting study of these early Negro writers has been made by Vernon Loggins and published under the title, *The Negro Author: His Development in America.* New York, Columbia University Press, 1931. $5.00.

verse which bears up interestingly under comparison. As a Negro writer she is placed in an almost echoless solitude. She had no followers; her patterns were Ovid and the English classicists who inspired her contemporaries. The vast bulk of her poetry was personal and non-racial; she indited lines "To the King's Most Excellent Majesty," "To His Excellency General Washington," to Neptune, and to Mæcenas, and to numerous friends on the death of relatives. A magnificent exception she was in this period of almost universal Negro illiteracy. When she went to England in 1773 she considered it wise to arm herself with attestations by Governor Thomas Hutchinson, John Hancock and some others, that she actually wrote the poems ascribed to her.

George Horton, during the early part of the nineteenth century, was composing verse which he could not even set down in writing. He nearly bought his freedom with the love lyrics which he composed for students of the University of North Carolina to be used among the young ladies of the vicinity. Assisted to literacy by some of the professors of the school, he published, in 1829, a volume of verse, *The Hope of Liberty,* and later numerous hymns. One of his brief poems will bear quotation here:

> Come, melting Pity, from afar
> And break this vast, enormous bar
>   Between a wretch and thee;
> Purchase a few short days of time,
> And bid a vassal soar sublime
>   On wings of liberty.

A Preface to Racial Understanding

Like strange, broken voices, writers of verse appeared, some thirty or more notable ones, between Wheatley and Dunbar. Among these Frances E. W. Harper of Baltimore occupies a preeminent position. The institution of slavery and its supporting theories grew. The attempts of the Negroes to express themselves were a struggle, without equipment, against the fast crystallizing philosophy of their sub-humanity and against arguments drawn from the very Scriptures which these people revered. Those writers who, after long silence, followed Phillis Wheatley, thought in terms of vital racial rebuttal. When Benjamin Banneker of Maryland prepared his Almanac, with its involved calculations, he sent the manuscript to Thomas Jefferson, praying that his accomplishment might be of some help in removing the general notions about his race.

The articulate Negroes were compelled to establish first their humanity. And so it was that the period just prior to the Civil War by its intensity turned practically all expression into the channel of personal experiences of fugitive slaves which, in themselves, held greater immediacy and dramatic power than either poetry or fiction. These made valuable material for the abolitionists to whose insistence may be accredited the preservation in record of many of these stories. Some are shot through with bright threads, and, despite a frequent crudeness, they have occasional passages of real beauty. Jessie Fauset, one of the modern Negro writers, was inspired to a poem by this brief paragraph from the autobiography of Sojourner Truth which seems to catch naïvely in its lap the vast tragedy and unutterable longing of those held in slavery:

"I can remember when I was a little girl, how my old mammy would sit out of doors in the evenings and look up at the stars and groan, and I would say, 'Mammy, what makes you groan so?' And she would say, 'I am groaning to think of my poor children; they do not know where I be and I don't know where they be. I look up at the stars and they look up at the stars!'"

Such narratives continued even after emancipation, being in their later form a more sophisticated revolt against the subtler limitations upon status.

The *Life of Gustavus Vassa,* the intrepid African, was published in England in 1789, and in America *The Story of Richard Allen* (founder of the African Methodist Episcopal Church) appeared in 1793. William Wells Brown, both in his personal narrative and in his *Clotel,* an attempt at a novel based upon a dramatic story of real life, revealed an uncannily alert and sensitive mind and an impressive command of English. Henry Box Brown, J. W. C. Bennington, the fugitive blacksmith, and Samuel Ringgold Ward had stories more powerful than their styles; but Frederick Douglass, the greatest of the fugitives, lacked neither style nor story.

These personal narratives steadily broadened from vicarious experiences to attempts to express group aspirations and emotions. They were yet a vital part of this literature when Booker T. Washington's *Up from Slavery,* a story of universal appeal, appeared, and they reached their highest art in the magnificent and bitterly intense *Souls of Black Folk,* by W. E. Burghardt DuBois, which appeared in 1903.

Emancipation ushered in a new phase of life and expression. With their "paper freedom" these people set out to copy the gloss of their surrounding culture, rebelling against every symbol of their so recent enslavement. Except for the fading light of a few brilliant survivors of the crisis, nothing of any consequence was produced until Paul Laurence Dunbar. Coming at that dark period when, with the release of the working classes, the independent struggle for existence had become more severe, Dunbar caught the picture of the Negro in his pathetic and contagiously humorous moods, accepted him without apology, and invested him with a new humanity. More, he made him likable—this simple, kindly, joyous creature, with his soft musical dialect and infectious rhythm. William Dean Howells, in an article in *Harper's Magazine,* hailed Dunbar as the first to feel Negro life esthetically and express it lyrically. Dunbar became a poet of folk life, mentioned in the same breath with Robert Burns. He lifted Negro poetry to a level of critical appreciation, lit new fires of hope among Negroes, then died, broken and disappointed that the world, ignoring his loftier, unrestricted verse had

> . . . turned to praise
> A jingle in a broken tongue.

The acceptability of Dunbar's dialect verse, however, inspired a host of followers, few of whom captured the convincing spontaneity of his poetry. Daniel Webster Davis, of Richmond, Virginia, seems to have achieved Dunbar's style most successfully in his volume of poems published under the title, *'Weh Down Souf.*

This period produced one outstanding novelist in Charles W. Chesnutt, who wrote and published five volumes before 1906, realistic stories and novels of the Reconstruction period, stories of that highly charged world of mixed blood relations across the line of race. Then his pen fell silent, although he lived for thirty years after the first publication.

The years between 1900 and 1915 were years of restlessness and uncertainty and transition. Hesitatingly at first, later with greater daring, Negro writers struck a note of frank discontent ranging in temper from bitter resentment to Christian forbearance. Frequently their verse was freighted with racial woes; and occasionally they spoke in terms of universal appeal. They discarded dialect because of its limitations, their technical command improved, their work had the authentic ring of poetry. Joseph S. Cotter, father and son, James Weldon Johnson, Leslie Pinckney Hill, Fenton Johnson, Edward Everett Hawkins, Lucian B. Watkins, Georgia Douglas Johnson, Anne Spencer, Charles Bertram Johnson, Alice Dunbar Nelson, Roscoe C. Jamison, James D. Corrothers, William Stanley Braithwaite, Jessie Fauset, and Angelina Grimké, a notable array, began that interesting tradition which blends the expression of the race mind with a refined equipment.

James Weldon Johnson's poem "The Creation" most vividly symbolizes the transition from the folk idiom to conscious artistic expression. Aside from being one of the most moving religious poems in American literature, it achieves a rare craftsmanship. In naïve, non-dialect speech, it blends the rich imagery of the uneducated Negro minister with the finished skill of a cultured Negro poet. In a curious fashion it bespeaks the meeting and parting of the old and new in Negro life in America.

> And God stepped out on space,
> And he looked around and said:
> I'm lonely—
> I'll make me a world.
>
> And far as the eye of God could see
> Darkness covered everything,
> Blacker than a hundred midnights
> Down in a cypress swamp.
>
> Then God smiled,
> And the light broke,
> And the darkness rolled up on one side,
> And the light stood shining on the other,
> And God said: That's good! . . .[1]

The new school of Negro writers really marked a profound reorientation of the race to the American scene, and they began to make contributions of undeniable worth in terms that could be promptly appreciated by literary critics without applying the racial yardstick. Dr. Robert E. Park has said that a people that is producing poetry is not a people that is per-

[1] From *God's Trombones,* by James Weldon Johnson. Copyright 1927 by The Viking Press, Inc., New York.

ishing. On the contrary, it is a people that is astir with vital impulses, a people inspired by life-giving visions. As with nationalist struggles in Europe, the new orientation of the Negro expressed itself in what has been described as a Negro renaissance, beginning shortly after the World War.

The most brilliant of these writers was Countee Cullen, who, as the *Manchester Guardian* observed, has contributed some of the loveliest lyrics of our day. He is well schooled in classic literature, and has a gift of epigrammatic expression. His latest work, after an interlude in fiction, is a translation of Euripedes's *The Medea*. Included in the volume are some of his own poems. He has published four volumes of poetry, a novel, and an anthology.

Claude McKay, a Jamaica-born poet, was really the first authentic voice of the new writers. It was he who first revealed that appraising detachment which could recapture the dark beauty of his own people and reveal it in a universal language. Sterling Brown, now professor of English at Howard University, whose volume of poems, *Southern Road,* was published in 1932, has the rich background of English literature and an unquestionable affection for Negro folk life. Langston Hughes, who has published two volumes of poems, several smaller volumes around a central theme, and a novel, *Not Without Laughter,* reflects a deep race consciousness. He strikes out boldly into new rhythms and into the folk life of the Negro in its new urban manifestation, so well characterized by the "blues." More recently he has reflected an industrial class consciousness in his poetry. He continues one of the significant figures of this period. Following the general tendency in American literature, practically all of these writers of poetry have in most recent years turned to prose.

The writers of sustained fiction have been few, the writers of drama, fewer. Walter White's *The Fire in the Flint* is a powerful story of a Negro family in a Southern town, balked into a sombre tragedy. *Flight,* a second novel by the same author, is concerned with the vicissitudes of a Negro girl who "left" the race and returned. W. E. Burghardt DuBois in 1911 wrote an epic of cotton, *The Quest of the Silver Fleece,* which was obviously foretimed. It is, however, one of the two books by Negro authors translated into the Russian language. The other is René Maran's *Batouala.* Jessie Fauset's novels, of which *There Is Confusion* was the first, have been an attempt to depict the life and fortunes of the educated Negro middle class. She has published four novels, the last of which was *Comedy, American Style.*

In this field, as in poetry, newer writers have abandoned the futile attempt of trying to correct the outward stereotypes of Negro life through the alchemy of reversing the color of their heroes and villains. They are pointing their plows in the virgin soil of their own life; and they are beginning to make it interesting. Rudolph Fisher's short stories have breathed life into the migrant Southern and West Indian Negroes in New York. George Schuyler has added satire to the themes. Of the earlier short story writers, Zora Hurston has perhaps gone farthest. Her interest, originally in Negro folk life, turned to a deliberate study of it. A result has been two volumes,

Jonah's Gourd Vine and *Men and Mules,* both genuinely entertaining and both soundly based upon real folk tales painstakingly gathered from over a wide area. Claude McKay's *Home to Harlem* was one of the first Negro novels to attain a high sales volume. Later novels like *Gingertown* showed real maturity and skill. Arna Bontemps, in addition to the novel *God Sends Sunday,* has done two books for children; one of these is *You Can't Pet a Possum,* and the other is *Popo and Fifina,* a story of Haitian child life done in collaboration with Langston Hughes.

The almost universal concern with social problems has precluded excursions into the field of belles-lettres. There has been, however, writing of a marked character with these very problems and group aspirations at the base. One thinks of DuBois's *Darkwater,* of the penetrating essays of Kelly Miller, in his two volumes, *Race Adjustment* and *Out of the House of Bondage.* Of great importance, not merely to Negro literature but to the spirit of the new creators of it, was *The New Negro,* a collection of poetry, fiction, and essays, edited by Alain Locke. It continues to be for the stranger to this new Negro life and thinking the portal to a new world of adventure.

The most recent prose writing of Negroes has been on serious sociological and economic themes, and these volumes, as a rule, have been based upon careful researches. Social criticism has also been notable in the present period, some of it reflecting doctrinaire economic points of view.

In art, with the possible exception of Henry O. Tanner, who

early went to live abroad, the Negro artists have tended toward the hard realism of modern art. Conspicuous among these artists are Aaron Douglas, whose symbolic figures depicting Negro life have their best presentation in the mural decorations of the new library at Fisk University; Hale Woodruff and Archibald Motley, Jr., painters; Augusta Savage, Meta Warrick Fuller, and Richmond Barthé, sculptors. A rich vein of talent in painting and sculpture has been uncovered largely through the work of the Harmon Foundation.

These notations of the work of Negroes in various fields are merely an acquaintance excursion into less familiar areas of accomplishment. Their work, interesting in itself as an expression of their own heritage and skill, is a part, however small, of that growing current which is the life of America.

CHAPTER SIX

SOME PORTRAITS OF NEGRO AMERICANS

BIOGRAPHY can serve two excellent purposes. It can reveal a personality, interesting in itself, in some of the color and warmth of real life; and it can reveal, through a personality, some of the social environments and forces which shaped it or were shaped by it. It is impossible to know the Negro without knowing some individual Negroes; and when individuals are known well enough, the chances are that the fact that they are Negroes will be less important than that they are men and women. The brief sketches which follow are intended to serve both of the purposes of biography. They are taken almost at random from a large list of busy people who are not only interesting to know but well worth knowing.

CHARLOTTE HAWKINS BROWN

It is a fairly common belief that a Negro born or reared in the North cannot work successfully in the South. The Negro may find it difficult to fit into the expected patterns, and the South itself expects the outsider, sooner or later, to forget himself and thus make endless trouble for all concerned. A Negro woman carefully educated in a New England atmosphere, vigorous and outspoken in ringing Yankee accents, sensitive to suffering, intolerant of ignorance and slovenliness, and with a crusader's temperament, would not be well advised, as a first suggestion at least, to go into the South to express her burning zeal.

The point of this sketch is that Charlotte Hawkins did go South in 1901 and built a unique and one of the most useful educational institutions for Negro youth in the South. She kept her vigorous outspoken spirit and Yankee accent and her sensitiveness to everything beautiful, and at a public testimonial meeting in 1930 she heard the South's first citizens call her a great and useful woman. But the real story lies within the years which marked the bitter, burning ordeal of getting acquainted.

Born in Henderson, North Carolina, in 1882, Charlotte Hawkins was taken by her parents a few years later to New England. They settled in the strange and cold environment of Cambridge, Massachusetts, lured to this corner of the North by the remembered graces of the women who came into North Carolina after the Civil War. Living in Cambridge was different from living in the simple though uninspiring security of at least a measure of food and shelter in a little Southern town. Life was hard because the father lacked a special skill to demand good pay and the family income suffered. They had moved North with the vague but persistent hope that the daughter might receive a good education and some of the graces associated with it. Since there was not enough money, the daughter went to work as a nurse girl, before and after school hours.

The New England schools once made a great point of Latin, and it happened to be Virgil that the girl was reading one day as she pushed the baby carriage. On her way she met a very interesting woman. Alice Freeman will be remembered first as a dean at the University of Chicago and later as president of Wellesley College during important formative years. She later resigned, married Harvard's Professor George Herbert Palmer, and lived in Cambridge. Mrs. Palmer liked the dark, eager girl with her Virgil and her job and baby carriage, and she engaged her in conversation. This chance meeting was the beginning of a long and beautiful friendship, and, for that matter, of Palmer Memorial Institute in North Carolina. The real education of Charlotte Hawkins also began with this meeting. From the tutelage of Mrs. Palmer she went to the State Normal School in Salem, Massachusetts, where she prepared to teach. Resourceful, skillful, and quick to learn, she had a passion to be at useful work which kept her impatient with the routine of formal preparation.

On one of her trips from Boston to Salem she met another stranger, and from this meeting came the suggestion which launched her on her work. According to her own story,

". . . A kindly faced elderly woman was attracted to me, and chose to change her seat that she might enter into conversation. I was one colored girl in a large group of young white girls, thereby the more conspicuous. Through conversation she discovered my aim. She told me of the work of the American Missionary Association in North Carolina, and its great need for well prepared teachers. . . ."

The American Missionary Association soon heard Charlotte's story and employed her. It was a fulfilment of her mother's dream when she went back, even though a stranger, to their native North Carolina. Going from Massachusetts to North Carolina was, after all, a serious step to take impetuously. Her picture of North Carolina was a romantic one. Children would be as eager to learn as she was to teach them. No one could doubt a sincerity which she felt so completely. But it was really Cambridge that had provided the romantic memories, and home was hard realism. As a protégé of the Palmers she had known the Eliots, the Cabots, the Lowells, and the daughters of Longfellow. They had cheered her eager return to her people, her idealism and her unquenchable hopes for her race. And then in October, 1901, she reached Sedalia, North Carolina, her station.

The North Carolinians resented this brown Yankee schoolmarm who tried "to put on airs." She could be no good influence, they said, for the children might imbibe her "social equality" ideas and make trouble for themselves. The school was not a school but a perilously dilapidated church. The teacher's cottage was not a cottage but a crumbling log cabin. The first chapter of Charlotte Hawkins's career ended when she tried to change things. Her white neighbors had cold and suspicious attitudes from the beginning, but she counted on the sympathetic support of the Negroes. When she mentioned getting a school building, however, the congregation that owned the church chilled and lost interest. Mrs. Palmer died in 1902, and the American Missionary Association withdrew its support.

Independently, Charlotte Hawkins set about to build a school as a memorial to her friend. A first building would cost about eight hundred dollars. She contracted for the building and journeyed hopefully north in the summer to solicit funds. One week in Cambridge and she fell ill and remained in the hospital until a week before the opening of her fall school term. Defeated, she began a sad return, but stopped in New York to follow up a vague last hope. She called on Mrs. Charles Guthrie, afraid that her dream was to be shattered. Unexpectedly Mr. Guthrie gave her the entire eight hundred dollars, along with the family's good wishes. A first tiny building was erected, which she promptly named Palmer Memorial Institute.

In 1917 this school celebrated its fifteenth anniversary. Friends journeyed from all parts of the country to join in the exercises. Hoping to place the school on a basis more secure than that of uncertain subscriptions, Charlotte Hawkins (now Charlotte Hawkins Brown) set about raising a partial endowment. Julius Rosenwald became interested and offered a generous annuity for five years. On a cold December night a fire reduced the industrial building and the commissary to ashes. The children, who had toiled with her dangerously to save the buildings, stood weeping over the ruins. Then she said: "These things God has given us, and we will build again."

Despite the completeness of this calamity, it had its compensations. Mrs. Brown's prompt plans to rebuild convinced her white neighbors, finally, that her mission in North Carolina was to build and not to destroy. When news of her misfortune reached Greensboro, Edward Wharton, a prominent banker, the chairman of her board of trustees, asked her plans for the future. She had won the good will of responsible Southern men but dared not hope for more. Remembering the loyal friends of her youth, she said, "I am going back to Boston to see if I can raise money to continue the school for the year." To her amazement Mr. Wharton answered, "You will not need to go to Boston to continue this institution. The people of Greensboro will advance money for the rest of the year." A meeting was planned, and on a Sunday afternoon she met a South which she had never known before. When she returned to Sedalia in the evening she had one thousand dollars in cash and pledges amounting to ten thousand dollars for the school's support and rebuilding.

The work went on. In 1920 Alice Freeman Palmer Hall was erected at a cost of a hundred and fifty thousand dollars, and there was laid the foundation for the present modern institution. Money came for other buildings, but these brought increased costs of maintenance. Mrs. Brown presented herself and a school safely through the long ordeal of its founding, to the American Missionary Association. The Association would take over the institution and share the responsibility of its upkeep, it said, if Mrs. Brown would raise a hundred and fifty thousand dollars more for buildings and a hundred and fifty thousand dollars for current expenses, payable thirty thousand dollars a year. The trustees and friends of the school considered this a polite refusal, but the undefeatable Charlotte Hawkins Brown turned quietly to the task and met the terms. It was later decided that the school would continue independent of the American Missionary Association.

Palmer Memorial Institute today *is* Sedalia. Much of the magnificence of the institution comes from the fact that it is the sturdy memorial to a friendship. The children who go out from it carry the deep markings of the personality that reared and nurtured the institution, and of the spirit that inspired it, which the founder will not let go.

What of the woman herself and the friends she made? Charles W. Eliot of Harvard served as chairman of the school's board of directors and of its endowment fund, always giving freely of his friendly advice and sage counsel. The Galen Stones of Boston at periods bore the principal burden of the school's financing. Julius Rosenwald helped surmount serious obstacles. Mrs. Charles D. McIver, famous North Carolina educator, served as the institution's sponsor in the South.

Booker T. Washington once remarked, in a moment of high good humor, "Well, Charlotte, you are about the only Negro convert I made in New England." President Franklin D. Roosevelt and Mrs. Roosevelt head the list of sponsors of the George Herbert Palmer Memorial Fund. After twenty-five years of teaching, Mrs. Brown secured a year's leave of absence and received the bachelor's degree at Wellesley. Her neighbors, Livingstone College, North Carolina College for Negroes, and Wilberforce University, have conferred honorary degrees upon her.

This is a record in which any American would take pride. But in the record also are many indignities which are the peculiar heritage of a brown face. The average American is spared the collapsing humiliation of having normal impulses and steps in line of duty blocked by petty functionaries, eager to impose the customary sanctions. Charlotte Hawkins's Yankee "brogue" and heavy erectness of spirit survived stabs that would have downed brittler determinations. She winced when it became necessary to telegraph friends in a certain hotel to meet her and escort her through the barricades set up by the hall boys. She knows the smell and mortification of freight elevators. Once a hotel porter directed an elevator boy to "carry her to the cellar," while a generous benefactor was waiting for her in one of the parlors at his invitation. It is a safe and teasing sport for elevator operators, once they have a Negro passenger who presumes to ride a passenger car, to carry him up and down, past his station again and again, until he becomes resigned in angered despair. As recently as 1935, in the company of a representative body of American educators, who offered to purchase the space of an entire Pullman car in order to spare her another humiliation, Mrs. Brown put on a maid's cap and apron so that she might ride through

Texas in the same car with her white friends. Not even the intercession of a friend, a former Secretary of the Navy, could win this courtesy from the railroad conductor.

The dark Yankee schoolmarm, with an ideal that never faltered, won the confidence and affection of her suspicious neighbors, endeared herself and passed on her vision to a thousand young hearts, and, besides, built a magnificent school.

JOHN HOPE

This sketch of the life of John Hope was completed just before the news was received of his sudden death in February, 1936, in his sixty-eighth year.

It is one index to the personality of John Hope that all through the last years of his life no one mentioned him as the dean of Negro educators. But that is what he became after the passing of Booker T. Washington. The attributes of venerableness and erudition which are associated with this honored position were persistently obscured by his refusing either to grow old in mind or scholastic in his wisdom. Here was a man who, so far as the public knew, suddenly blossomed into lively maturity after his sixtieth birthday, undertook the consolidation of three historic Negro educational institutions, accomplished the impossible physical feat of grouping several score of scattered buildings in Atlanta into an organic unity, created a distinguished faculty for the first graduate school among the Negro colleges, and induced the government to wipe out the slums that had massed around the Negro schools.

A Preface to Racial Understanding

But life had not really begun for John Hope at sixty; this was only another flowering. For forty years he had been quietly building into Negro youth qualities of character that were rich and real; almost every Morehouse man reflects the personality of this great teacher. Quiet of voice, contemplative, with swift intuition, a sense of humor, and, most important, a genius for blending great philosophical principles into the raw energies of youth, he seemed to be able both to measure and to spur to its limits every variety of ability.

During the early history of the Negro college in the South, when the more vocal leaders were debating the kinds of education Negroes should have and great campaigns of physical expansion were abroad, John Hope was a silent, familiar figure, usually about but always preoccupied, it seemed, with some problem too serious to let go, too intimate and particular to make a speech about. This problem was invariably, we now know, a deep-lying personality difficulty of one of his students, and he was trying to devise some constructive solution. He seemed content, for his part, to build obscurely the most intangible of institutions—a spirit of intelligent service and a love of truth, deep in the foundations of lives of these friends of his, who were his students. One result of this is that at present five of the most useful heads of Negro institutions are men whose careers were shaped by his hands. Mordecai Johnson of Howard University, John P. Watson of Arkansas State College, John W. Davis of West Virginia State College, W. R. Banks of Prairie View, and Benjamin T. Hubert of Georgia State College, were his students. These men and their work would be testimony of the spirit of a great teacher, if he had been nothing else.

John Hope was born in Augusta, Georgia, June 2, 1868. He received his elementary education in Georgia and entered Worcester Academy in Massachusetts in 1886. The fact that he was a working student, earning all of his expenses, did not prevent him from sharing the school activities and winning popularity among his fellow students. He became editor-in-chief of the student monthly, and, at graduation, was both class historian and commencement speaker. In 1890 he entered Brown University, from which he was graduated in 1894. Then he returned to Georgia to begin his career.

The missionary associations, which were the main support of Negro higher education in this period, were seeking well trained teachers for their schools. It was upon these teachers that they depended to build the colleges which they did not then have but which now are an accomplished fact. The American Baptist Home Mission Society sent John Hope to Roger Williams University at Nashville, Tennessee, and later to Atlanta Baptist College, now Morehouse College. The young teacher's power to inspire his students, as well as his executive efficiency, was shown during the sixteen years he spent in the classroom. In 1906 he succeeded Dr. George Sale as president of Morehouse, the first of the Negro presidents under the great missionary boards.

For his simple, quiet, character building and steady advancement of education Dr. Hope received recognition in the field of education without seeking the dubious acclaim of a public too readily fascinated, at times, by the public gestures of leadership. Many different institutions conferred on him the degree of Doctor of Laws: Howard University in 1920; Bucknell University in 1923; McMaster University in 1928, on the occasion of the World Baptist Alliance Congress in Toronto, at the same time that that university honored ten other outstanding Baptist leaders of the world; Bates College in 1932; and Brown University, in 1935. These were the tributes of the educational world to a great educator.

In 1928 he was selected as one of the thirty-five delegates from North America to attend the meeting of the International Missionary Council at Jerusalem. The following year he received the Harmon Award for distinguished services in the field of education.

He was never lured from his one dominant concern of building men to advertise his opinions on education. The published articles about him contain no learned dissertations by him on educational theory or race problems, but such fragments of his rich philosophy as could be captured by a student and set down. The addresses which best reveal him are not the public ones, but the intimate unannounced talks to his students.

"And I have come today to ask you this question: Are you willing to sacrifice enough of the material things in life? I have come to ask you if you are willing to make a sacrifice of material things in order that you may guarantee to yourself a release of those higher forces, those higher qualities, that you possess and which, through your education, have become so actively and consciously present that it would be a hard matter for you to live them down."

These talks were not compounded of involved doctrines but of simple truth "crashed thunderously through open doors." In fertile young minds seeds were planted that are still growing sturdily in many communities far from Atlanta. John Hope talked to the students quietly and interestingly about the problems that trouble young minds. Not even the best of them can always find a personal philosophy early, and they are likely to despair of having something that is not feelingly their own. He warned them against taking themselves too seriously, against borrowing formulas which they neither felt nor understood.

"I know that you can't do anything now, as you say. But let me make this request of you: do not let your inability to do anything about it now worry you. Do not let it dictate too much what kind of courses you are electing. . . . Get all the advantages and enrichment you can. When the time comes for you to get your diploma, be physically strong and intellectually welcome in any institution you wish to attend. Keep your thinking processes healthy so that you will be able actually to discover with your mind. Be fine and spiritual, so that your intellectual processes will get the urge and direction and vitality they ought to have."

John Hope, after nearly forty years of quiet work in education and religion, began life again at sixty when he undertook the direction of the most ambitious educational program for Negroes in the South. Only then was his full stature revealed.

Dean of Negro educators, he represented the most advanced outlook in the educational field.

DR. VIRGINIA ALEXANDER

The woman who invades a sphere traditionally reserved for men does so only with great effort. When a Negro woman enters such a field she has the double handicap of being a Negro and a woman. It is not remarkable that Dr. Alexander became a successful physician. There are ninety-two other Negro women practising medicine, and doing well. What gives to her, still a young woman, a unique distinction is the deep social concern that dominates a fine mind, a superb skill, and a radiant personality.

Virginia Alexander was born February 4, 1899, in Philadelphia. Her father was Hilliard B. Alexander, the owner of a riding academy there. Her mother attended Wayland Seminary in Washington and was guided for years by that gentle scholar, Dr. G. M. King, who had left New England to teach in the South. She was a rural school teacher in the South before she married. Virginia was four years old when her mother died, leaving five children. Into the world of this girl only a few years beyond infancy there came with her mother's death a sense of heavy responsibility, compounded of childish fancy and real life. She tried to take her mother's place in the household. Schooldays came, and her protective impulses reached out to other children who needed friends, help, food, encouragement. Good scholarship was incidental to the obligation she felt to help these children. When she completed her elementary work in 1913, however, she was on the list of honor students, and was treasurer of the class. Her high school work at the William Penn High School was completed in three and a half years. She was president of "Populus Romanus," on the school paper for two terms, judge in the Student Court, active in the Mathematics Club, the Athletic Association, and the Social Worker's Club. A well rounded person.

There was a local character who influenced the girl profoundly. She thanks "Brother" Moore, pastor of Zion Baptist Church, which she attended, for an inspiration which never left her. This Baptist preacher was unusual in his social vision and community interest. His sermons were frequently devoted to practical advice to his parishioners to keep their kitchens as clean as their parlors; to keep their underclothes and topcoats as clean as their dresses; not to cover up odors with perfumes and powders; not to sham and lie at all, but "especially not in the presence of children." He tried to make members of his church community consciously aware of their responsibility for delinquent children. He went to court and pleaded for his boys; he founded a boys' band, to keep his bad boys, whom he himself would not call bad, off the streets. He tried to create community clubs, mothers' clubs, and a recreation center; and he made his young people vocal. Virginia Alexander was one of these young people. She says when she was seventeen years old Brother Moore left Philadelphia with the firm belief that someone would "come out of Zion" and put his teachings into practice.

While she was still in high school her father lost his business and the prospects of college faded. Some students were given tickets to see a play called "Experience" and were asked to write a paper on it. The sponsor of the contest was struck by the young girl's intensity and insight and gave her first prize and a promise of one hundred dollars a year toward her college education. She completed her college work in three years. This was near the end of the World War. A Philadelphia mother, in her joy over the safe return of her son from the war, established a medical fellowship and tried to place it where it would best express her social purpose. It went to Virginia Alexander for study at the Women's Medical College of Pennsylvania.

The spirit that had made so many friends met its real challenge in this college. Hard study and outside work to supplement her scholarship, and the cold unfriendliness of her surroundings, bore down heavily, eventually affecting her health. By graduation time she had overcome most of the race prejudice and was about to relax again into her first passion for people when the problem of an interneship arose. Where women were acceptable, Negroes were barred; where Negro men were acceptable, women were barred. She was advised by the head of the institution that received many of the graduates of her school not to take the examination. Even if she ranked first in a thousand applicants, she was warned, an appointment would not be given. Finally, the Kansas City General Hospital suspended its rule against women internes and admitted Dr. Alexander and her classmate, Dr. E. Mae

McCarroll, in July, 1925. In the summer of 1927 she began her practice.

A first obligation was to repay the loans that had supplemented her scanty means during the years of study. This included personal loans by the sponsor of the contest on "Experience," with whom she had left her insurance policy as security. In the spirit of repaying society for the good fortune of some fellowship aid, she tithed her income to help other medical students. Then she was free for the work to which she had consecrated all her youthful strength and eager enthusiasm.

It was during her junior year in medical school that Dr. Alexander came to know the Negro section of North Philadelphia, a dismal area of wretched homes, disease and delinquency. One of her schemes for earning money had been selling Christmas cards and insurance policies. This contact helped her to a practical interest in public health.

Dr. Alexander's present concern is not so much in private practice as in public health. There are, however, no public posts for Negroes in this shamefully neglected field. So she supports her own public health work with returns from her practice. Underprivileged children are her major concern. The mothers of the area worship her; they pay her nothing, because they have nothing to pay.

This is how her time has been spent since 1927. She is a staff member of the Frederick Douglass Memorial Hospital and Nurses' Training School, the Hospital of the Women's Medical College of Pennsylvania, Pennsylvania Hospital, and is a member of the board of management of Convalescent Hospital. She holds membership in the Philadelphia County Medical Society, the Pennsylvania State Medical Society, and the Academy of Medicine and Allied Sciences. Her interest in social service has been shown in her membership on the board of management of Wharton Settlement. In the Young Women's Christian Association she has served as chairman of the board of management of the Southwest Branch, and as member of the city-wide board. She is a member of the Philadelphia board of the Women's International League for Peace and Freedom, and is a former member of the national board of this organization. She belongs to the Religious Society of Friends and is a member of its Race Relations Committee and of the Board of the Institute of Race Relations. She has been a member of the executive committee of the Young Friends Movement.

In 1930 she opened the Aspiranto Health Home in North Philadelphia, where nearly one-third of the Negro population live under most dismayingly poverty-ridden conditions. It is not a hospital but a big home to which mothers come, where normal maternity cases are handled, tonsilectomies are performed, heart patients are admitted for rest, nourishment and general medical guidance, and where the children under her wise supervision get the close attention and expert care they need.

She is now waiting for medicine to be socialized. She is socializing her own practice and she is profoundly happy in it.

Some Portraits of Negro Americans

MAUDELLE BROWN BOUSFIELD

The constant pressure of the race problem makes serious demands upon Negro educators. They must enter public life and become the interpreters of the aspirations of their people, across the chasm of race. It is as difficult, usually, for a Negro to develop professionally in the general field of teaching as it is for one to interpret successfully the problems of Negro education. Mrs. Maudelle Bousfield is interesting because she is one of the most accomplished educators in the public school system of Chicago, the first Negro woman to be made principal of a Chicago public school, and of a school in which only a portion of the children are Negroes.

Such advancement in the system was by no means a matter of routine promotion. The odds are usually against either normal promotion or accidental elevation of Negro teachers beyond the post of teacher. With the visible handicap of color, a Negro must have a margin of technical excellence sufficient to overweigh a great variety of possible social objections. Mrs. Bousfield began her career as the first Negro woman to graduate from the University of Illinois, and she was the first Negro dean of girls in the Chicago school system.

Maudelle Brown was born in St. Louis, Missouri, in 1885. Her father was a school teacher, and belonged to the post-Civil War generation of Negro teachers who entered the profession with a religious fervor to improve the status and condition of Negroes through education. For more than fifty years Professor Brown taught in the schools of Missouri, ending his career as principal of L'Ouverture School in St. Louis. Her mother was a niece of Bishop Benjamin Tanner of the African Methodist Episcopal Church, and a cousin of Henry O. Tanner, the celebrated painter. Growing up in a progressive family, the girl had the advantage of an accumulated professional tradition.

Her father was a teacher, but he was receiving a Negro teacher's salary. When the girl began to direct herself to this field there were four other children in school. Her contribution to reducing the cost of tuition was in increasing her course load and completing her work in the preparatory school in St. Louis in less than the required four years. There were few Negroes attending the University of Illinois when she entered in 1903. A pleasing personality and a clear, crisp scholarship won for her the friendship of her associates and the respect of her instructors. She reduced tuition costs again by completing the four year course in three years.

Her first position was teaching mathematics in a Baltimore high school; then she went to Chicago, where she continued her instruction in this subject at the Wendell Phillips High School, which at that time was attended by comparatively few Negroes. The subject of mathematics is not usually the most popular one in a high school. The discovery of her real school effectiveness grew out of a rare ability to create enthusiasm in this subject, and to build, at the same time, internal disciplines of lasting quality among her students. Marriage to Dr. Midian O. Bousfield, a physician now prominent in public health work among Negroes, and the birth of a daughter, limited her duties to the home for eight years. Then she returned to the high school. After four years more of teaching she became a dean of girls. The University of Illinois *Alumni News* pointed with pride to three such of their own who had been entrusted with this post in large school systems.

As dean of girls she was responsible for all the social life of the school, extracurricular activities, and the personnel work entailed in adjusting pupils' problems and directing character education. Her mastery of the tremendous task of the relationships of white and Negro students, and her successful handling of the problems arising among pupils recently migrated from the South, were a triumph of skill and social insight. In 1928 Mrs. Bousfield was appointed principal of the Keith School, and after a complete reconstruction of the school, which included its physical expansion, she was transferred, in 1931, to the Stephen A. Douglass School.

It is impossible to remain long in her presence without feeling the calm, sturdy personality of a master of the profession. Both white and Negro children feel it, and, more often than not, forget to think of her race. It was impossible to ignore her talents when the system required, for two different situations, a sure and resourceful person.

Aside from her success in the schoolroom, Mrs. Bousfield has given of her time and experience to useful organizations related to her interests. She has encouraged and participated in sororities, infusing new enthusiasm for their ideals of scholarship and character. Along with this, she has organized parent-teacher organizations and has been active in the National Negro Music Association and the Central Association of Science and Mathematics. Moreover, she found time to complete work at the University of Chicago for the master's degree. There has been little that is externally spectacular about Mrs. Bousfield's career, but it has been a clear enough demonstration to young Negro girls that professional excellence can steadily push forward across even the most difficult frontiers.

ROLAND HAYES

Few American singers have been able to command the sustained enthusiasm that has been accorded Roland Hayes. For twenty years his popularity with discriminating music lovers has swept along unabated. To attend one of his recitals has become a rare esthetic indulgence, an institution, almost a rite. The brief, even obscure, notice of his appearance in musical circles has been sufficient to pack Carnegie Hall in New York City. He has been the one artist forced by a riotous acclaim to turn his back upon a full auditorium audience and sing to other hundreds packed in behind him on the huge stage of New York's greatest concert hall.

Roland Hayes is interesting quite as much for the lowly condition from which he emerged as for the brilliant eminence which he has reached. Pictures of his youth show that he was of the Negroid type that might be encountered in any Negro quarter. The years of living his music have molded his features into an almost mystical cast, the embodiment of the deep emotional quality of the spirituals which he loves so well and expresses so completely. He well expressed this new personality when he said:

"If, as I truly believe, there is purpose and plan in my life, it is this: that I shall help my people to use what has been given to them; that I shall have my share in rediscovering the qualities we have almost let slip away from us; and that we can make our special contribution—only an humble one, perhaps, but our very own!—to human experience."

This purpose and plan he has carried out with a magnificence of spirit that has drawn the admiration of the world.

The Hayes family were tenant farmers in Georgia, near Curryville, some distance even from a railroad. There were no schools for Negro children close enough to be attended by the three children in the family, and there was no prospect of an education beyond the meager instruction of their ex-slave parents. It was hard enough with all of them working to maintain themselves. An accident eventually crippled the father, and later he died, forcing upon the mother and children the hard work of plowing and planting and picking cotton, along with keeping house. For three years after the death of the father the family struggled against mounting odds to keep alive. Finally the mother, aware that the children were condemned by circumstance and their environment to ignorance and poverty, decided upon a bold break with the farm. Packing their few belongings, they walked the long highway to Chattanooga.

A Preface to Racial Understanding

In this city Roland, then fifteen, found a job handling iron in a sash-weight factory. Within a year he had been advanced to foreman of his gang and earned three dollars a day. This was unheard of money for the family. He studied evenings to overcome some of the early lack of schooling and attended church, where he discovered that he could fall into the singing of the audience easily. There was in the town a young Negro graduate of Oberlin College, Arthur Calhoun, who became interested in his voice, which seemed to have possibilities. Calhoun urged the young singer-worker to go to school and improve his voice along with his mind. At first the suggestion was preposterous; the income was too esential for the family, and Roland was far behind in the grades. A wise mother, however, softened these apprehensions, gave him fifty dollars she had saved, and sent him to Fisk University in Nashville.

At Fisk he began his course of study, finding employment during the summers in various surrounding cities. Chance carried him to Louisville, Kentucky, where he worked as a waiter at the Pendennis Club. As was inevitable, some of the members had occasion to hear him sing informally. Nothing happened beyond the casual entertainment of the moment. He sang for a period with the Fisk Jubilee Singers, under the direction of John Work, senior. On one occasion in Boston, when he was appearing with these singers, a white man who had heard him at the Pendennis Club was in the audience. Interested, he took the opportunity with the help of other friends to arrange for Hayes to study with Arthur

Hubbard, one of the best known voice teachers in the country. From this point on his attention was directed to the concert stage.

His voice, under the hand of a master, began to reveal more of its natural charm. But this required funds for more study. He gave concerts in Negro churches and schools that thrilled his Negro audiences, but he could not meet the exacting financial terms of a concert hall. Several efforts failed, but finally a last venture in Symphony Hall in Boston, in 1918, yielded enough surplus to carry him abroad. Here he studied and traveled and finally made a first London appearance. When this was followed by two command appearances before King George and Queen Mary, his reputation was established.

Thereafter he was eagerly heard over Europe, and his return to America was a triumphal one. The concert halls were opened to him and were packed with admirers. Hayes never disappointed them, either in the perfection of his music or in the charm of his manner.

When we think of Negro singers we usually think of a voice, with the beauty and power of that voice transcending all such limitations as race, lack of training, and fine feeling for interpretation. The most successful of the Negro singers specialize in songs peculiar to their race, thus combining a racial with a musical experience. Roland Hayes has in some respects a limited voice, but he sings with an artistry which is rare on American concert platforms. Over against the vogue, set by Caruso and the operatic tenors, of a grand heroic style, he uses a finesse and a subtle effect which few singers have achieved.

Along with the Negro folk songs he gives authoritative presentations of the highest type of French, Italian and German art songs. He has almost succeeded in making German *lieder* popular. His diction and enunciation are perfect, baring no trace of his Southern background. This is evidenced in the fact that he has been most successful in each country when using the native tongue of that country. He received highest acclaim, for example, for his beautiful interpretation of "La Rêve," the dream song from "Manon," in Belgium, where a Belgian tenor had established his reputation in singing this same song. Though he does not stress Negro folk songs exclusively, he sings them with true and moving interpretation. Many critics who were startled at the prominent position he so quickly won for himself gave various "explanations." Deems Taylor exploded, to his own satisfaction at least, the theory that Roland Hayes's success was due to the phenomenon of a Negro's singing accurately in foreign languages, rather than to any high degree of artistry. He went to one of Hayes's recitals, kept his eyes closed throughout the recital, and judged him from the pure effect of his singing on an impersonal listener. After this experience the critic proclaimed Roland Hayes a complete artist in every sense of the word.

The importance of Roland Hayes transcends his personal triumphs. He has provided the emotional and esthetic experiences in which new racial appreciations have been born.

Some Portraits of Negro Americans

It would be as ridiculous as it would be barbaric, in such a moment, to quibble and insist upon maintaining the abstract dogmas about race and the Negro's traditional place in American civilization.

CHAPTER SEVEN

THE NEGRO AND THE CHURCH

THERE are two important aspects of this question to be considered: the attitude of the organized church toward the Negro, and the attitude of the Negro toward the organized church. In the first instance the issues involved are implicit in the historic relationship of the church and slavery; in the second instance the issues are those which created and still maintain the one outstanding social institution of the Negro in America. In this chapter it is the purpose to discuss the church as a social institution that reflects the social attitudes and sentiments of its members and of its age.

An age-old conflict between the interpretation of religion through the organized church and the social behavior inspired by this interpretation, has centered around the question of the relationship of the church to social issues and to social values. These values have not always been the same and are not now the same everywhere. Whatever the doctrine, it is difficult for the adherent to it to escape the subtle influence of custom or the social institutions in which he is born, or to escape being dominated by the prevailing conception of these values themselves. Organized religion may be seen as conserving, through the church, the existing social values, or it may be seen as constantly creating new values. It may be regarded as supporting the mores, or as preserving only those values in the mores that foster the highest possible human relationships.

It must be assumed that the social and political character of the church is determined by the people themselves, and that this character has relationship to fundamental Christian principles only to the extent that the church is able to translate these principles into Christian behavior. Otherwise, it would be difficult to explain the extraordinary contradictions which are a part of the social history of the organized Christian church. It has given sanction to those high moral codes by which alone society could achieve wholesome and well ordered life. At the same time, it has given sanction to social institutions which were, in themselves, inconsistent with these codes. It has been, unquestionably, the greatest and most persistent force in the propagation of a high faith among the peoples of the world, and it has been at times, because of uncourageous leadership, among the least powerful of the social institutions in great moral crises. It has produced some of the greatest moral leaders of every age, and some of the most conservative and undaring of spirits committed to the service of mankind. It has contributed some of the most uncompromising forces in the age-old struggle of mankind for social justice, and it has at the same time set up some of the strongest forces of resistance to change. It frequently has reflected economic and political forces, and just as frequently it has changed them; it has varied its sanctions to fit new conditions, and it has inspired new social conditions by sanctioning new values. In all, the church has been one of the most powerful forces in the history of Western civilization.

No circumstance so well illustrates this dual rôle of the church as the history of slavery itself. It was an earnest desire for the conversion of the heathen that resulted in the first contact of Europe with the Africans, who were later to experience such a varied fate at the hands of Christian nations. The first and most audacious of the early British slave-ship captains under Queen Elizabeth was Sir John Hawkins, who sailed forth in 1562 on his mission in the good ship *Jesus*. In spite of this brusque disregard of the moral amenities by a rampant commercial age, there were persistent evidences of religious sentiment. The tremendous economic factors that helped to crystallize the institution of slavery in America were constantly being undermined by individual expressions of religiously inspired humanitarian sentiment. Throughout the history of slavery there was no enforcing legislation that was not weakened by the accumulated effect of individual manumissions, inspired by consciences made sensitive by the philosophy of Christianity. For every law enacted that fixed more firmly the lowly position of the slave, there were scores of slaveholders who became convinced of the moral wrong of the institution, and set their slaves free. At the beginning of the Civil War there were nearly half a million free Negroes.

The Negro and the Church

Indeed, there were almost as many free Negroes as slave owners.

THE COLONIAL CHURCH AND SLAVERY

The spreading of Christian doctrines went hand in hand with the colonization of the New World. At the very beginning it was the inspired pity of Las Casas, the Spanish priest who came over on one of Columbus's journeys, that prompted a request for Negro slaves when he was convinced that the Indians could not adjust themselves to the rigorous demands of New World exploration. In the early English colony in America, slavery was condoned because it was a means of Christianizing the heathen. When conversion, theoretically, freed the slave, economic expediency dictated a change of view on freedom itself. The Church of England, when appealed to in the crisis, gave a judgment through the Bishop of London that "Christianity would make the least alteration in civil property; that is, the freedom which Christianity gives is a freedom from the bondage of Sin and Satan; . . . but as to their outward condition, they [the slaves] remained as before, even after baptism."

The conflict between the Christian principle of brotherhood and the fact of human slavery led to a denial of brotherhood. If it was wrong to enslave a brother then it would be more comfortable to believe that the Negro was not quite, though almost, human, and thus, not quite a brother. There were also numerous volumes providing a "Bible defense" of slavery. One important argument employed was put thus: "Man is made in the image of God, and since God, as everyone knows, is not a Negro, it follows that the Negro is not a man."

Church policy has varied with the interpretation of its leaders in the light of social expediency. It has both opposed slavery and owned slaves. The Church of England, which became established in America ahead of the Methodists and Baptists, found its support very largely among slave owners. It was but natural that in common policy it would reflect the sentiments of the slaveholders when the issue of slavery became political. Much of the scientific opinion of that day supported the view that the Negro belonged to a sub-human race, the "point at which man and brute most closely approached each other."

The Baptists and Methodists, who began a serious missionary campaign in the middle of the eighteenth century, addressed themselves to the common people and sought black as well as white converts. Slave converts multiplied at a rapid rate. At first a common spirit of worship permitted meeting in the same church. Religious teaching and enlisting of converts went on even as the economic fears of owners made Negro meetings for worship increasingly difficult, and as the churches themselves began to discourage the presence of these Negroes in the common meeting places. As early as 1787 the pattern for the slave gallery was established and spread rapidly as the solution of the social side of religious worship.

Between the defense of slavery and its active condemnation there was a body of men, in and out of the church, who moved along in the current of the tradition, against their deeper convictions. Even so illustrious a character as Patrick Henry of Virginia wrote to a Quaker, in 1773, that he regarded slavery "as repugnant to humanity as it is inconsistent with the Bible, and destructive of liberty." In explanation of his continued use of slaves, he said, "I am drawn along by the general inconvenience of living without them."

The Quakers were consistent in their opposition to slavery and began, as early as 1675, in Virginia and Maryland, a crusade against the institution. They made their appeal to the universal conscience of mankind. From this group came many of the outstanding anti-slavery leaders and the organizers of the Underground Railroad. There were individuals in the South who, when they failed to get the active support of the church organizations, joined the Quakers in order to oppose slavery. Sarah Grimke, the daughter of a South Carolina judge, was one of these, and to her strong anti-slavery sentiments is credited the *Appeal to the Christian Women of the South* which appeared in 1821.

THE CHURCH DIVIDED

Despite the growing economic importance of slavery, there was always in the South a group of religious leaders who set themselves against the institution. Among the Presbyterians were the Reverend David Rice of Kentucky as early as 1792, Samuel Doak of Tennessee, and the Reverend John Paxton of Virginia. The Baptists had a vigorous representative in the Reverend David Barrow of Kentucky, author of a widely

circulated anti-slavery pamphlet, and the Reverend Joshua
Carman of Virginia, who boldly opposed Christian fellowship with slaveholders. One association of Baptists in Kentucky separated themselves from slaveholders and denounced
slavery as "a sinful and abominable system." A general conference of the Methodist Episcopal Church in the South
as early as 1784 declared slavery "contrary to the law of
God, man and nature, and hurtful to society," and in 1812
another conference actually barred slaveholders from becoming local elders.

Once the institution became firmly and definitely established, many of these voices were stilled and new voices
within the church were raised in an involved defense of an
indispensable economic institution. Religious bodies in the
North continued to condemn slavery with impunity, to the
growing embarrassment of their Southern membership. They
had no acute problem immediately connected with slavery,
since it had not proved sufficiently profitable to support it
in the North. By 1833, a violent change of view could be
noted in the South, where the issue was real and immediate.
It began to be evident that the political and economic sec-
tionalism which found expression in general social policies
also influenced the general policies of the church. Immediate
emancipation, it was felt, however desirable theoretically, held
dangers to the white population as well as the slave population. The agitation of the abolitionists thus had the effect
of combining every class of men, Christian and unbeliever,
to hold them in close bondage for common safety. In 1844

both the Methodist and the Baptist churches divided sectionally on the slavery issue, and shortly afterwards they were
followed by the Presbyterians.

The general attitude adopted by the Methodist Episcopal
Church, South, after 1833 was that slavery was not an institution of the church but of the state, and that the church had
no right to interfere with it. The first General Conference
which met at Petersburg, Virginia, in 1846 passed these
resolutions:

"We wholly disclaim any right, wish or intention, to interfere with the civil and political relation between master
and slave; we consider the subject as having been put beyond the legislation, by the general government, as well as
the control, of ecclesiastical bodies; the only safe, scriptural,
and prudent way for us, both as ministers and people, is
wholly to refrain from agitating the subject." [1]

At no time, however, despite the terrific pressure of the
slavery institution upon this church, its modification of its
first position regarding the right to hold slaves, and the
rupture with the Northern church, has it diminished its interest in the welfare of the Negro, slave and free. The
strength of the sectional breach is made more evident in the
fact that the Baptists separated completely at the same time,
although each local church is by policy autonomous.

The complete separation of the church organizations on
a racial basis today makes interracial contact in worship an
extremely rare occurrence. In the North the Negroes are

[1] *Journal of the M. E. Church, South, 1846,* p. 75.

not particularly welcomed in and are not notably eager to attend the white churches. A few mixed congregations, however, still exist. In the South, with few exceptions, Negro worshipers would have difficulty being admitted at all to churches with white memberships. The same difference of opinion and of conscience appears in the present-day church on the issue of race that existed before the great schism of the churches. So far as the South is concerned, it is largely those activities lying in the field of education that bring the white churches into contact with the Negro population. In this service practically all denominations have shared to some extent. The significance of the deep social division between the churches lies in the fact that the two races are deprived of the one great institution through which contact and communication are possible.

The Work of the Missionary

Perhaps the greatest contribution of the church to Negro development has been the missionaries. They were the culture bearers for a race newly released into the responsibilities of freedom. Almost immediately following the outbreak of the Civil War, thousands of Negro contrabands began pouring into the towns from the rural parts of Virginia and North Carolina, constituting a new kind of problem. They were unlettered, homeless and propertyless, and the forerunners of several million more who were to follow.

The American Missionary Association in 1861 sent out the first missionaries. This was the beginning of a great movement which eventually included all the great denominations in an enterprise which, perhaps more than any other factor, is responsible for the rapid progress of the Negro since slavery. The men and women who devoted their lives to the cause of Negro education were representatives of the best in the American culture. Money could not have bought the service of the scholarship and general intellectual maturity which they gave in such fullness to a very human cause. There were those who deserted posts in great universities to work patiently and hopefully with the untutored minds of these children of slavery. It required a sturdiness of character and a deep religious faith to make of this adventure a mission worth while. They gave to the institutions founded with church support a character which they retain even today.

The withdrawal of the Southern churches over the slavery issue was clearly a reflection of the social pressures generated around the issue. It had the effect of stimulating aggressive effort in the evangelizing of slaves, despite differing opinions on the question of immediate emancipation. In many instances, white pastors ministered to separate congregations. After the war these activities gradually broadened to include a number of different types of work. In 1899 the women of the Methodist Episcopal Church, South, finally turned frankly and directly to the Southern Negro work as the most pressing field for their labors. This marked, also, a shifting of the chief focus of attention from remote foreign fields to home missions. The work of these women in developing Paine College in Augusta is an outstanding example of the church's

heightened concern. Individuals offered themselves and their
life services to the cause of Negro education and religious
and social service.

In 1912 the first social settlement for Negroes was established
at Paine College. Settlements in Augusta, Georgia, Nashville
and Memphis, Tennessee, Birmingham, Alabama, Spartan-
burg, South Carolina, Winston-Salem, North Carolina, and
New Orleans, Louisiana, have supplemented the educational
work in the schools. Today the Bethlehem Center in Nashville, which is supported by the Methodist Episcopal Church,
South, has, in addition to a useful and devoted staff, the
services of a number of students of Scarritt College, where
a course on race relations is offered. Their work in the Center brings them closely into contact with the Negro community with its myriad social problems, and in the Center
they work side by side with Negro students from Fisk University who are preparing themselves, similarly, for useful
service.

The Protestant Episcopal Church, through its American
Church Institute for Negroes, maintains nine schools, among
which are the excellent Fort Valley Normal and Industrial
School in Georgia and St. Augustine's College in Raleigh,
North Carolina, with its associated school for social work,
the Bishop Tuttle Training School. In the North the famous
Robert Gould Shaw House, in Boston, was established in
1908 with the support of the Episcopal diocese. While not
exclusively for Negroes, it specifically planned for and encouraged their inclusion.

These social activities of the churches can only be sketched. Not all such work has been brought to the attention of the public. This suggests the importance of examining the programs of individual churches for their services in this field.

THE NEGRO CHURCH

The Episcopal church in America did not break away from the Church of England until this country was separated politically, following the American Revolution. Although there were recurring expressions of interest of the church in the conversion of the slave, there was little real sentiment for fellowship with him in holy communion; and conversion to Christianity for the slave remained a matter quite apart from church organization. John Wesley, the great Methodist leader, who had been deeply affected by the writings of Anthony Benezet, was opposed to slavery as was Roger Williams the Baptist, although they lived at different periods. Both sought converts among the common people.

This general background helps to explain the interesting development of a separate Negro church organization within the shadow of several strong denominations. Ordinarily, the Negroes who worshiped at all, prior to this separate organization, attended the regular churches and sat in special pews, until the expedient of a separate gallery was hit upon. The number of worshipers was small, and even these were a social problem. A serious dilemma faced the religious leaders. They were under moral obligation to convert the slaves and at the same time under serious pressure not to receive them into the church when converted. As a result few churches were eagerly active in building up a congregation of Negroes, and those who sought converts welcomed any device that might remove the embarrassment caused by their presence in the churches.

The first Negro church, thus, was a purely local branch of a white Baptist church and was established in Silver Bluff, South Carolina, about 1773. This was followed by another Negro church in Yamacraw, Georgia. George Leile and Andrew Bryan were the first notable Negro ministers, and they are a part of the dramatic history of the Negro church in America. The organization of these scattered churches antedated by more than twenty-five years the African Methodist Episcopal Church.

The personality best remembered in the development of the Negro denomination is Richard Allen. He was born in Philadelphia in 1760 and became an itinerant preacher and communicant of St. George's Episcopal Church in that city. Interested in the welfare of his people, he sought to draw them into the church, to the great discomfiture of the congregation. The Negroes were segregated, but made no complaint. At one meeting, according to Richard Allen, he and a friend, Absalom Jones, who became no less famed for his religious work, were kneeling in prayer when they were approached and pulled from their knees by a trustee of the church. After they had been frankly told that they were unwelcome, they were compelled by force to leave the church. In indignation and protest they founded an independent church in which Negroes might worship. When most of its members decided to retain affiliation with the Episcopal communion, Allen and some of his friends withdrew and set up a Methodist body, out of which developed the African Methodist Episcopal Church. Richard Allen was consecrated its first bishop in 1816 and Absalom Jones, who in the meantime had become rector of St. Thomas's Church in Philadelphia, participated in the ceremonies.

The democracy of the Baptists, during their beginning years in America, permitted mixed congregations. There are several instances of Negro pastors of white congregations in this early period, and there were white pastors of Negro congregations. When, however, the Baptists were assured of acceptance through the grant of toleration in the United States, concern developed over the status of the colored brethren. In 1841 the Negro Baptist Church in Richmond, Virginia, was constituted by the withdrawal of 387 white members, leaving 1,708 Negroes in a church of their own. In 1844, when the Methodist denominations separated sectionally, there was created another Negro church organization, the Colored Methodist Episcopal Church.

Subsequent subdivisions of denominations have increased the number of Negro church organizations, but the fact remains that the church has proved a vital institution for the Negroes. Blocked off from virtually all other channels of expression, members of this race have found in the church their one outstanding social institution. It has provided a substitute for political organization and has furnished a channel for social as well as religious expression; it has been the center for face-to-face relations, for communication, for recreation, and for physical as well as psychological escape from their troubles. It has been welcomed by Negroes even in areas where physical separation in worship was not demanded.

The Negro church has until recently provided the leadership and internal control for the great masses of the Negro population. During slavery the Negro preacher was the first and only professional worker among Negroes. But he has been considerably more; he has been the interpreter of values for the Negro group, moral, ethical and social. He has been the leader, the idealist, the link with the future on earth and beyond it. Similarly, the church has been the one Negro institution tolerated by the surrounding society. Neither the school nor the political institutions, nor even, in some instances, the family could stand as inviolate as the Negro's church. It became the great common ground for spiritual growth and instruction, and the most important, if not the exclusive, channel through which impulses to group sociability expressed themselves. It continues today a tremendously strong institution, although the natural broadening of the Negro's sphere of life has permitted his taking a larger part in other activities of the general community.

In 1930 there were 25,034 Negro clergymen. In the states with more than 50,000 Negroes, the average number of Negro persons for each Negro clergyman ranged from 251 in Kansas to 717 in Mississippi, while the average for the country as a whole was 475. This indicates that for their respective populations there are twice as many Negro as white clergymen. Dr. William A. Daniel, in his study of the education of Negro ministers, points out that the educational qualifications of these ministers are not on the whole very high, and that only 3.7 per cent of the 1,011 students enrolled in Negro seminaries in 1923 and 1924 were college graduates. Benjamin E. Mays and J. W. Nicholson, in a further study of the Negro's church made in 1933, noted that few college men are looking forward to the ministry as a career.

The Negro church is feeling the effect of this undertrained ministry in positions which by their very character hold considerable power and influence. Less than twenty per cent of Negro clergymen hold academic or theological degrees; yet in spite of this dearth, few candidates for the ministry are being graduated from the colleges. It appears that the younger generation, for one reason or another, is avoiding the ministry and, to no little extent, the church itself.

The census of religious bodies, made by the federal government in 1926, provides interesting figures on the finances of the churches. In that year 39,245 Negro churches reporting, with a membership of 5,203,487, expended $43,024,258. These institutions contribute to Negro education, give individual charity, and help to finance missions and social movements, but the great bulk of the expenditures go into buildings. It appears, from such records as have been made available, that the Negro population is "overchurched" so far as buildings are concerned, and that a disproportionately high amount goes into additional buildings. For greater efficiency in the expenditure of the small earnings of communicants who support these institutions, there is little question of the correctness of this observation. If, however, one may draw inferences from present trends, the larger churches, although as a rule better managed, are not always the most satisfying. In the frequent splitting of churches and the appearance of small and somewhat unorthodox religious groups, there are, perhaps, factors responsible other than the simple desire to create a new pastorate, or to conclude a doctrinal disagreement.

The vigor and enthusiasm of these small churches indicate a revolt against the too rigid conventionality of some of the larger institutions. If this means a new invigoration of religious life, there is much that can be said for the tendency. However, the leadership is yet open to question. The transition from rural and small town life to city life, the successive social crises which are the lot of the Negro everywhere, carry with them the demand for the intimate offices of a mothering institution, such as the church has always been for the Negro. The situation in general presents to the Negro church a real challenge which grows out of the changing status of Negro life itself.

So valuable have been the social benefits of the church to the Negro that objections have been raised by Negro churches themselves to a policy of unification with white churches. The leaders fear the double threat to the prestige and independence of the present ranking church officers in separate organizations, and to the comfort of communicants, who are not now bound to expose themselves to common racial prejudices in worship.

These Negro church organizations have made themselves responsible for the support of a number of schools. Their funds are less adequate than those of the controlling boards of the large white church denominations and, as a result, the schools frequently fail to reach the same educational standard. They have, however, wielded as important an influence upon Negro education, within their limits, as upon the morale of the Negro group in America.

THE CHURCH AND INTERRACIAL COOPERATION

There has been a natural transition for the social-minded leadership of the church from purely missionary service to interracial cooperation. The very measure of success of the educational programs which they have supported has helped to bring about this change. Moreover, in a rapidly changing world the possible field of service has broadened of itself, from simple religious instruction and relief of destitution involving individual Negroes, to a consideration of those social problems which restrict the wholesome expansion of Negro personality. The outstanding leaders in the South, in organized attacks on social injustice in race relations, have been ministers and church leaders, acting with or without the support of their church bodies. Certain of the women's church organizations have taken the boldest stand of any group in the South against mob violence and lynching, and they are the chief support of the active interracial committees.

A Preface to Racial Understanding

The fact cannot be escaped, however, that the leadership of the majority of the churches in the South has remained silent on all of these evils, regarding them as of none of their concern. The Federal Council of Churches recently sent a minister into several communities in which lynchings had occurred, to find out the attitude of local ministers. In one community there had been an agreed policy among the churches to say nothing at all about the affair. In the sermon of one of these ministers on the Sunday following a particularly horrible lynching, he exhorted his congregation to have "more of the kind of love that will help in work across the seas to bring Christ to those who do not know." In still another community a minister explained: "I have been laboring for the saving of lost souls, and my duties in this His work are so heavy and confining that I have not time or adequate ability, I am afraid, to be of any help."

The pressure of local sentiment has been enough, frequently, to intimidate many of those whose convictions may have lacked only the courage to express them. This is illustrated in the case of the minister of an important church in a community in which a lynching was seriously threatened, who refused to make a gesture of disapproval lest he should "lose his influence with the people." The instances of serious compromise with the Christian ideal are by no means confined to the South. When the minister of a New York church locked the doors against Negro worshipers and tried to defend his action, one nationally read commentator was prompted to this challenging observation:

The Negro and the Church

"Here in a dramatic form we have a test of the sincerity of organized Christianity. In spite of the stalwart stand taken by a few preachers here and there, it seems obvious that the average professing Christian of today has not the slightest intention of attempting any actual experiment in living the life suggested by Jesus."

The issue of race has undoubtedly created the greatest social challenge to the church since its founding in America, and it constitutes today a supreme test of the strength of Christian faith. Just as the church has been, throughout a stressful period of America's history, the testing ground for a great moral issue, so it is today the one common ground for social reconstruction.

CHAPTER EIGHT

THE CONQUEST OF RACIAL PREJUDICE

RACE problems are so familiar to most Americans that it is usual to assume that they arise out of fundamental instincts and are inevitable. A little reflection, however, will reveal that there can be "race problems" whether the question of race is involved or not. For example, before the Civil War the non-property-holding whites of the South, called "poor white trash," "crackers," or "clay eaters," were regarded by the landed gentry as innately inferior, although they came frequently from the same racial stock.

We often hear individuals ascribe to race certain failings which are universal. The ordinary man on the street, with little knowledge of history and less of anthropology and biology, nevertheless feels himself perfectly competent to pass a judgment on an individual which is based upon racial prejudices. On the other hand, there are those who are unwittingly gracious to individuals until informed of their racial connection. A fundamental racial instinct should not depend upon chance belief and other people's opinions!

The Conquest of Racial Prejudice

There is, however, a deep-lying human trait which expresses itself in those situations commonly recognized as racial. When two groups with different backgrounds come together, there is, almost always, a conflict of interests. In the case of the Negroes in America, the conditions which governed their first relations with the white population were rigidly prescribed and firmly fixed. They were to be a permanently subordinate group, serving wholly the interests of the stronger group. All the social institutions, the laws, and the general public opinion were rooted in this assumption.

There was no race problem during slavery, because there was no serious questioning of this fixed relationship on the part of either the slave or the slave owning class. Slavery is the most "efficient" form of accommodation between two dissimilar peoples. But slavery is today so abhorrent to enlightened societies that it is no longer tolerated as a social institution. Moreover, slavery would be economically disastrous in a machine civilization, even though many persons continue to enjoy the personal thrill of commanding other people's lives and exploiting their labor.

A race problem developed for the first time when the fixed social position of the Negro slave was changed by his emancipation. So long as complete subordination, even in a theoretical state of freedom, is never challenged, a race problem can be escaped. But citizenship brings demands for education, sound health, security, and self-support, demands which in turn mean competition for work and the chance to earn a living. At every step in the new freedom of the

Negroes new conditions and new problems had to be met, and for these there were no such ready-made and final solutions as slavery provided. At each step new adjustments and compromises had to be worked out between the group seeking to dominate, to maintain a fixed sphere, and the group seeking to increase its citizenship privileges by getting "out of its place." So long as this continues there will be a race problem.

It is, perhaps, because our form of government, in principle at least, is democratic, that so many conflicts arise between what every citizen has the right to expect, and what it is deemed expedient for the Negro citizen to have. Their former status as slaves, together with a habit of thinking about them as permanent inferiors, no doubt have considerable influence upon present-day race relations.

ASSIMILATION VERSUS REPATRIATION

Back of most of the problems is a reluctance, for one reason or another, to consider assimilation as desirable. The question of assimilation, whether cultural or biological, is one about which the layman knows actually very little, but this does not prevent him from having strong opinions on the matter. At any rate, these circumstances have contributed to the thinking of those persons who feel it incumbent upon them to control these relations rationally.

The first important racial philosophy of action to be formulated under the new circumstances brought about by emancipation was the quite drastic one of expulsion. This expulsion did not always carry the implication of violence. Always the economic demand for Negro workers tended to modify such political expedients as were suggested, and where this factor was not present it was most often preferred that the separation should be brought about by mutual consent. Colonization thus came to express the most satisfying solution of the race problem.

The idea of the repatriation of the Negro population in Africa first appeared with the spread of abolition sentiment before the Civil War. In a short while there developed a great variety of proposals, and from a wide range of inspirations. Interestingly enough, the most determined programs for the colonization of Negroes arose in the North, along with the philosophy of political integration which provided the chief arguments for the abolitionists. There did not exist unanimity on the issue of political integration even among the staunch abolitionists.

Two distinct motives, however, were back of the programs for Negro colonization. One of these was the desire that Negroes should find a new environment, free from the social handicaps of America, in which they could develop to manhood's stature unhampered. Another was the more calculating concern of some of the early statesmen for getting rid of them. Although seeking the same objective, the distinction in motive would more appropriately brand the former as colonization and the latter as deportation. The Negroes themselves were divided in their own philosophy regarding colonization as a solution of their problems.

A Preface to Racial Understanding

MOVEMENTS FOR BETTER RACE RELATIONS

In the South, notably, the opposing philosophies on the race question became more articulate. One group, which tended to regard the existing rôle of the Negro as fixed and natural, saw no reason for disturbing this order of things. The other group, which recognized the serious handicaps of the Negro and the anomaly of the existence of such a class in a democracy, felt conscience-bound to bring about some improvement in Negro status. They believed that this could be done without serious violence to the accepted policy of racial separation. This latter group, however, were seriously handicapped in carrying out their benevolent intentions. The smallest gesture of practical concern for social justice promptly exposed them to the charge of encouraging social equality. Because this phrase was so highly charged emotionally, its very vagueness contributed to its terror; for it included anything from intermarriage to a deluge of barbarism and racial disintegration. Such a charge, then, was usually sufficient to cast the threat of social ostracism.

Gains were made, however, by the group of individuals who, as a practical expression of Christian principles, sought social justice through good will. Negroes began to make adjustment to various measures of segregation which permitted more or less peaceful existence so long as they accepted the position in the community vaguely described as "their place."

It was not until the beginning of the twentieth century, however, that public opinion permitted the full development of programs based upon a philosophy of improving race relations, and upon the cultural development of the Negro race. They began almost simultaneously in the South and in the North.

The first organization in the South which set out boldly to make the race problem a major part of its program was the Commission on Southern Race Questions, organized in 1912 by Dr. James H. Dillard, then of New Orleans. It drew its support from religious bodies and educational institutions and at first addressed itself more to the sympathetic study of these problems than to direct action. The Southern Sociological Conference, which came later, drafted a set of resolutions embodying certain new social convictions on the acute issues of race. These resolutions dealt with a wide list of injustices so gross and so obvious as to defy any challenge.

FOUR AGENCIES OF INTERRACIAL COOPERATION

These first pioneering organizations have now ceased to function, but their duties and policies have been taken over and expanded in other important organizations which are active today. The four organizations whose programs are primarily concerned with the race issues are (1) The National Urban League, (2) The National Association for the Advancement of Colored People, (3) The Southern Commission on Interracial Cooperation, and (4) The Department of Race Relations of the Federal Council of Churches of Christ in America. Three of these organizations have their headquarters in the North and one in the South, although all of them are active to some extent in both sections. Their membership is composed of persons of both races. The oldest of these is the National Urban League, which was one of the first to establish an interracial board of control.

1. In 1910 the Committee for Improving the Industrial Condition of Negroes in New York City and the League for the Protection of Colored Women united to form the Committee on Urban Conditions among Negroes in the City of New York. The following year a more unified organization was formed and given the name, National League on Urban Conditions among Negroes. From its inception the Urban League has recognized and tentatively accepted existing social alignments and has elected to work primarily with the Negro in an effort to improve his social and economic status within the social structure. With such a program it has thus avoided serious clashes with the community mores, has drawn the support of influential white leaders, and has secured the aid of industry itself, notably in the North, in improving the character and position of Negro workers.

Urban Leagues are now established in Northern and Southern cities. The organization reached the peak of its service during the large-scale migration of Southern Negroes to Northern industrial centers shortly after the outbreak of the World War. It made itself responsible for adjusting the acute social problems incident to this precipitous urbanization and took as its motto of service, "Not alms, but opportunity." Its program has been focused mainly on the economic problem, but a wide range of social activities, such as provision of better housing and recreational facilities, has been included. Its work has been confined to urban centers and mainly to the larger cities, which are in the North. While it has accepted the philosophy of internal improvement and group development for the Negro population, its aspirations and programs for Negroes have been such as to make them indistinguishable from the aspirations of American citizens generally. This latter policy has occasionally brought the organization into conflict with certain elements of Southern sentiment. The official organ of the Urban League is the monthly magazine, *Opportunity*.

2. The National Association for the Advancement of Colored People, with headquarters in New York, is one of the major organizations whose program is based frankly upon the philosophy of political and cultural assimilation. It was organized in New York City in May, 1910, and represents a merger of two groups formed a few years earlier. One of these was the Niagara Movement, inaugurated in 1905 by a group of Negro leaders who sought to make known their grievances and their desires for full citizenship status. The policy of this association, being based upon the principles established in the Constitution and its amendments, has been more aggressive than any other of these interracial bodies. In seeking to obtain for Negroes their legal rights and civic privileges, it has been necessary to combat public opinion and uncontrolled lawlessness, to carry on a persistent campaign of propaganda for Negro rights, and to seek redress of legal irregularities before the Supreme Court of the United

States. It has been responsible for establishing some important legal safeguards for Negroes and for focusing the attention of the country on the public crime of lynching. Because of its motivating philosophy and program the N.A.A.C.P. has been unpopular in the South, where these policies run counter to the mores of the section. The bulk of its white membership has been in the North and East. One indication of changing mores, however, has been the increasing acceptance of its policies and the increase in its membership within the South. Its official organ is *The Crisis,* a monthly periodical.

3. The Commission on Interracial Cooperation, with headquarters in Atlanta, Georgia, is the one outstanding organization in the South working to improve race relations. Its membership is Southern. It has worked for social justice and improved living conditions for Negroes, and has vigorously sought to bring about a more agreeable adjustment between the white and Negro populations in an area in which the traditional pattern demanded social segregation.

This organization came into existence immediately after the World War, when the South was disturbed, on the one hand, over the threatened social problems incident to the return of Negro soldiers and, on the other hand, over the economic threat involved in the draining off of Southern Negro workers for Northern industry. This general state of mind made possible for the first time the rapid expansion of a program of racial betterment long cherished by a few of the advanced social minds of the section. The commission, under the able direction of Dr. Will W. Alexander, began its program with such indisputable issues as mob violence; the gross municipal neglect which leads to disease and excesive mortality among the Negroes; legal injustices, arbitrary violence, and exploitation. Gradually it approached problems of racial etiquette, advocated joint service on committees dealing with these problems, and expanded its program of public education through the press. Still later, as it became recognized as an agency more to be respected for its social value than feared as a menace to the best of the social tradition, it was able to deal effectively with the question of lynching, the tenancy evil, and local official misdealings with Negroes. It has been able successfully to oppose the Ku Klux Klan, which, in its policy, represents in grossest form the philosophy of complete and fixed subordination of the Negro, in every phase of his life. The Interracial Commission has been criticized at times by certain other groups both for going too far and for not going far enough. Working within the mores, it has consistently pursued a policy of change which has not been too radical to weaken seriously its influence within its region.

4. The Federal Council of the Churches of Christ in America organized in 1922 its Commission on the Church and Race Relations, now known as the Department of Race Relations. Its purpose was "to foster through the churches of America interracial fellowship and cooperative action in accord with the ideals of Jesus Christ." The organization set for itself the broad task of removing old evils in the interracial situation in America, preventing new evils from de-

veloping, and integrating the Negro in American life. Actual programs have included sponsoring two national and numerous local interracial conferences, annual race relations programs in churches, and activities aimed at promoting economic and civic justice. It has been especially active in the campaign against lynchings, and early interested itself in the Negro tenant farmer in the cotton belt. These programs, directed from the New York headquarters, are given application through state and local church federations and denominational agencies.

The Y.M.C.A. and the Y.W.C.A.

The Young Men's Christian Association and the Young Women's Christian Association have interracial programs. In the main these programs consist of providing for the establishment of branch organizations for Negroes in cities with populations large enough to support them. Even in New York and Chicago there are separate Negro branches, although Negroes are not specifically barred from participation in the activities of the central association.

The interracial activities have generally been of an educational nature: encouraging joint conferences where race problems are discussed; presenting Negro speakers; and attempting to promote more amicable relations between the two groups. The type of work done by the local branches varies according to the community in which the association is located, since the membership is drawn from populations which reflect local prejudices and attitudes.

The Conquest of Racial Prejudice

The Young Men's Christian Association has in its national as well as its local organizations a separate structure for its work with Negroes. It aims at decentralization of control. The Young Women's Christian Association, on the other hand, has no separate Negro division in its national office, but has Negroes on both the National Board and the staff. Its local units are separated, with white and Negro field secretaries. While there are attempts by these organizations to improve race relations within their general membership through publicity and conferences, the principal work of the branches is to carry out a general program of character building, with the race problem as an incidental feature.

INTERRACIAL ACTIVITIES OF MISSION AGENCIES

The interracial work of the church missionary societies, discussed more fully in another chapter, is concentrated very largely in the South and is confined for the most part to educational ventures and to social work. Most of the church bodies support, or contribute to the support of, Negro colleges. Differences in these Negro schools reflect, in certain respects, the policies of the churches behind them. The social work has been carried on by the women's organizations of the churches, and the Methodist Episcopal Church, South, has been conspicuous in this field. They have established and maintained settlement houses and provided personnel from their number for actual service. The settlements provide recreation and social work in Southern cities where these programs are greatly needed. Such activities, while not attacking directly the basic race problems, do make a fuller life for Negroes and provide advantages for underprivileged communities which would otherwise be wholly lacking.

The Roman Catholic Church in America has evinced a continuing interest in the welfare of the Negroes, largely as a means of making proselytes. Under the Catholic Board for Mission Work among Colored People, schools are maintained and some social work carried on among the two hundred thousand or more Negro communicants. A journal, *The Interracial Review,* serves as an organ of general public information and guidance on the racial issue.

MOVEMENTS AMONG NEGROES

Apart from organizations of bi-racial composition devoted to the task of improving race relations and Negro status in the United States, there have been movements among Negroes themselves. These have been, in most instances, loosely organized and short lived. An example of such a movement has been the sporadic attempts of Negro groups to escape the tradition of their local areas by migration. The best known of migration leaders was Pap Singleton, who led large numbers of Negroes from Mississippi, Tennessee, and Georgia to Kansas in 1879. The Negro migrations of 1918 and 1922-23 were more or less leaderless and were of more directly economic motivation.

Shortly after the World War there arose another Negro movement which proved one of the most dramatic in the recent history of this race. This movement was organized as the

The Conquest of Racial Prejudice

United Negro Improvement Association, under the leadership of Marcus Garvey, a West Indian. It was, in its external organization, a colonization scheme which sought to accomplish for Negroes escape from America to a haven in Africa where they could develop an independent state. Although fantastic and impossible as a program, it drew into its ranks large groups of Negroes who had long been thwarted and disillusioned in their struggle for status.

The membership of the association came largely from the Negro masses of the North and South, and, while it did little towards finding its territorial haven, the movement provided a psychological escape for these masses from their troubles, and ministered to broken egos and long-suppressed desires for expression. The movement provided colorful uniforms, parades, meetings and regular periods of indulgence in a glamorous dream of establishing a great Black Republic. The public laughed at the Knights of the Nile, the Dukes of Uganda, the Black Cross Nurses, and the Black Star Steamship Line, created by the "Provisional President of Africa," but these extravagant fancies lost much of their humor as a mounting and menacing racial solidarity spread from the parent body in America to the West Indies and to the natives of Africa. Their leader was arrested for promising too much through the mails. He was sent to prison, and after a few years the movement collapsed.

Other similar movements have developed since, but without the glamor and success of the United Negro Improvement Association. The Pan-African Congress, organized and for a period directed by the brilliant scholar and writer, Dr. W. E. Burghardt DuBois, formerly editor of *The Crisis,* was the intellectual counterpart of the Garvey movement. It sought intellectual union and spiritual solidarity of the darker races throughout the world. The fourth Pan-African Congress met in New York City in 1927. One of the less notable of these movements was the Alaskan Colonization Branch of the United Congo Improvement Association, Incorporated, which had for a brief time headquarters in Cleveland, Ohio. Another is the "49th State" movement, sponsored by a group of young Negroes in Chicago. Still another is the African Reconstruction Association, which looks again wistfully to Africa. All of these have been chiefly emotional and sentimental safety valves, with little prospect of actual consummation. They have, however, made it increasingly clear that the race issue, if it is ever to find comfortable solution, will have to be worked out in the United States.

REALISM AND UNDERSTANDING

In consideration of actual approaches to racial problems in America, it is important that there be awareness of the wide variety of patterns of relations in the United States with equally varied backgrounds and traditions. Not only science but realism is essential if there is to be sufficient understanding to permit control. The orthodoxy of the South on the question of the Negro, whether morally wrong or right, is held in varying forms with all of the conviction and intensity and reality of morality itself. These beliefs change slowly and are scarcely, if at all, affected by factual contradiction or argument. The conclusions of anthropology, however sound, may not always be impressive. Such attitudes are a natural and logical expression of a culture, and, as anthropologists themselves agree, cultures change slowly; but they do change, and by processes which can be understood.

RACE PROBLEMS AND ATTITUDES

It may be useful to identify some of the racial attitudes and dogmas which so largely control relations. If these attitudes are grouped it will be noted that they tend to sift down to a few broad assumptions, accepted as so true as not to be questioned. First, there is the assumption that Negroes are mentally and morally inferior and that this difference, being innate, cannot be changed easily, if at all. Then there is the assumption that Negroes represent a backward culture and are constitutionally incapable of fully taking on European culture. It is also firmly believed that race consciousness, which includes fundamental antipathies, is a matter of instinct and as such is not learned. This is accompanied by the conviction that the incorporation of Negroes into the basic American culture carries the threat of weakening this culture.

These basic assumptions are most firmly held by those who have least studied the questions involved, and they vary in intensity among individuals and groups. They are, nevertheless, very real considerations and, because of their persistence and force, frequently prevent the first steps of action dictated by simple impulses to social justice. Where a course of behavior based upon these assumptions is well defined, any violation of the orthodoxy, even in the interest of a Christian principle, can provoke, as one man phrased it, "a scandal of public disapproval." There are phrases like "social equality," "the Negro's place," and "race intermingling," which, by their very vagueness, are freighted with high emotional content. Many sensitive individuals feel embarrassment over social injustices which they observe, but they hesitate to interfere lest they but create new problems of racial adjustment and control. The usual reaction is to make oneself believe that what exists as current practice, although wrong as an ultimate policy, is excusable as an immediate expedient.

Fear plays an important rôle, although it is usually denied that fear enters into these considerations. There is, however, fear of loss of security, fear of loss of status or group prestige, and myriad nameless fears. Seldom are the real motives back of group attitudes stated. They do not sound rational or civil. It is simpler to place a taboo on the discussion of such matters, or better still, to give these underlying motives other and more respectable labels. In the end separate group sentiments and antagonisms develop unmodified by personal experiences, and stagnant convictions persist.

Attention has been called earlier to the fact that changes in economic patterns may carry along with them certain broad changes in social and race relations. It is well to recognize that many of the present assumptions regarding Negroes had their origin in historical situations plausible enough to warrant them. The situations have changed more rapidly than the early assumptions based upon them. For example, the high illiteracy of Negroes in slavery, the irregular social habits which were a part of the institution, the devices for self-entertainment where avenues for cultural development were systematically cut off, could quite easily lend a semblance of truth to the casual assumption that their minds were dull and different, their morals loose, and their standards hopelessly depraved.

A pertinent example of the persistence of these old patterns appears in a contrast of the approved etiquette of race relations under slavery and the current definition of the Negro's place in society. The etiquette of slavery prescribed that it was not correct to use the title "Mr." or "Mrs." or "Miss" in addressing a slave. A pronounced courtesy was expected of the slave, and was, accordingly, the rule. Shaking hands was taboo, and when it did occur the slave could lighten the strain by first deprecatingly wiping his hands on his clothing. The "black mammy," who was a privileged character, kissed the children even after they were grown. The title of "captain" was conferred on all white men with whom the slave was unacquainted. Negro men whose advanced age and loyalty prompted some distinction from the younger ones or from strange "boys" were given the courtesy title of "uncle," and the older Negro women were called "aunt." No slave sat in the presence of the master or mistress and, if outdoors, none talked without removing his hat. Slaves ate in the kitchen, even out of the same frying pan in which the master's food was cooked, but no exchange of places was possible either in or out of the presence of one another. A place of honor at a funeral was given to house servants. In church slaves were seated in the gallery, if there was one, or they might have special services. Slaves were named after biblical, historical and mythological characters. Entering and leaving buildings, boats, or trains, the slave followed the master.

The list of social conventions under slavery could be expanded at great length, but the point is that these observances of the etiquette of slavery are still more or less expected of Negroes who are no longer slaves. Thus a Negro is considered out of rôle when for any reason this age-old and archaic tradition is violated. As with other traditions good or bad, violation carries the threat of loss of status, and this is most deeply resented by those least certain about their own status. The "smart Negro" is simply one who takes a different conception of himself from that defined by the tradition. In North Carolina one of the most prominent Negroes in America was attacked by a soft-drink dispenser because he ordered a soft drink to be consumed in the store. Serious personal conflicts may arise from trivial incidents. In response to this some Negroes employ a protective device of excessive flattery of whites and depreciation of themselves, to insure tolerance and security in a community. Other Negroes refer to them contemptuously as "uncle Toms."

The Passing of a Great Tradition

Despite the strength of tradition and a firm belief in many quarters in its utility, it is becoming increasingly clear that in clinging to outworn concepts in the field of race, backwardness is encouraged in other fields. This may be illustrated in a surprising number of ways. The racial tradition has had an unfortunate influence upon the development of social science, upon the principles of law observance and enforcement, upon art and letters, upon public education, upon public manners, and upon the practice of the Christian principle of brotherhood.

One need only note, for example, the early literature in the field of anthropology and sociology to be made aware of the extent to which the judgments of students were warped in the past by popular estimates of the mentality of the so-called backward races. In the field of psychology, until very recently students have reported great differences in innate mental, emotional and moral qualities. Eugenics became confused in a fog of political considerations regarding superior and inferior races. Other students have spent years seeking to find race differences in muscle systems, brain weights, and head forms. Although present-day anthropologists now insist that "there are no sure evidences of real racial differences in mental traits," the layman continues to think and act on the old assumptions.

In the field of labor, race consciousness has proved a serious handicap. The policy of exclusion of Negroes from labor organizations has weakened the effectiveness of these organizations and made impossible anything approaching a united labor policy. In making Negroes the underdogs of industry, labor reflects the same reckless callousness to human values which it has so loudly protested. There is scarcely any wonder that the emancipation of labor should mean to many American workers emancipation from labor, or that a common struggle for the privileges guaranteed by democracy should degenerate into a snobbish class struggle among workers themselves, aligning skilled workers against unskilled workers, and white laborers against black laborers. On such a shaky foundation it was inevitable that labor should lose faith even in itself without knowing why, when strength was most needed, and that membership in its organizations should decline.

In the matter of law observance and enforcement a truly serious situation is threatened for our most important democratic institutions. Respect for law cannot be encouraged where exceptions are condoned because of race. Thoughtful citizens have cause for concern over the state of affairs when the lynching of a Negro can be dismissed as no crime because it was "the will of the people." Injustice may begin with the Negro and escape censure, but the damage to the principles of justice can spread to weaken the entire structure of the courts. A colored boy in Vicksburg, Mississippi, stole a bicycle and was given five years at hard labor. A white boy, tried on the same day, was given two years for stealing $1,900. In Houston, Texas, a white waiter was fined $25 for illicitly selling liquor to soldiers. Four Negroes were fined $225 each by the same judge for the same offense. A white man in a Southern state who shot a Negro was given a nominal fine for discharging firearms within the city limits. The wisdom of Booker T. Washington's observation that it is difficult to hold a Negro in the ditch without staying there with him has striking pertinence.

It is to the great credit of the church that the most effective mass condemnation of lynching has come from its members. The Federal Council of Churches has kept the public aware of this evil, and individual churches and denominations have put themselves on record as opposing this practice in the name of humanity and the Christian ideal of justice and morality. In the Congressional hearings on the Costigan-Wagner bills, the most vigorous testimony was offered by church groups. Mrs. Jessie Daniel Ames of the Southern Commission on Interracial Cooperation has, as her chief allies in the fight against lynching, several thousand church women throughout the South, who have the courage of their faith to brave public opinion in the determined effort to end the evil.

Literature and art have been regarded as free worlds, but, as everyone knows, there are definite patterns apart from artistic merit which must be followed to be accepted by the public, and, consequently, by the publishers. These patterns take the form of stereotypes which enable the man in the street to recognize the type. The Negroes have had sound reason for objecting to being represented by certain stereotypes which publishers assure them are the only ones which the public will accept. Fortunately this restriction has been breaking down in recent years.

The cause of American education has been influenced by race sentiment. A question which delayed compulsory education in the South for many years, as indeed it delayed woman suffrage, concerned the inclusion of Negroes in this privilege. When it was eventually accepted, the compulsory aspect was, except in a few conscientious communities, simply ignored. The states least able to support education are bound by the tradition wastefully to maintain two sets of schools and, further, to balance the difference by diverting to one group of children, in such communities, a part of what belongs to another. Horace Mann Bond makes a very incisive comment on the practice in many states of so administering the funds for education that white schools get more and Negro schools get less than they are entitled to on the basis of a fair per capita distribution. He says that in such states the Negro child is the white child's surest asset in education.

The social amenities are greatly distorted by the race tradition. There is no more socially grotesque situation than that of a normally gracious personality forced to show rudeness to an individual of another group, merely to maintain a set of conventions. It is even more tragic when some gentlemen and scholars and even religious leaders find it impossible to accord simple titles of respect where such respect is earned; when taboos which do not have even the frail support of snobbishness can dictate discourteous social behavior; and when children are taught prejudices and even hatred which they would not otherwise feel.

The Christian church in America has not escaped the effect of race sentiments. Although much of the social reformation has been at the instance of religiously inspired individuals, there are churches which so adhere to the customs of the community as to ignore obvious social injustices in some instances and even give moral support to these injustices. Hopefully, social Christianity today places a stamp of censure upon laggards even of its own order, and the most vigorous religious bodies are finding a way of expressing their Christianity by work with their immediate neighbors.

The purpose of democracy is the minimizing of injustices and the universalizing of its gains. It may appear at this stage that any practical effort to make possible a fuller life for underprivileged groups would go against nature or would take ages for accomplishment. But human nature is plastic and social customs are mutable. In the midst of our present setting it is difficult to believe that our habits of thinking and our actions were radically different in the very recent past, and it is even more difficult to imagine that they can be different in the future. The fact that human nature is plastic and responds to social change is the one great hope which inspires the step-by-step progress of race relations.

In spite of the persistence of many old and strongly held views of race, it is possible to see changes. It is difficult now, for example, to take seriously the beliefs which were current only a few years ago and which molded and prompted behavior and all our social relations. In the field of religion we no longer burn witches. In the field of medicine we no longer cure asthma with the lungs of foxes, or find healing power in the moss from the skull of a person violently killed. We no longer keep women out of colleges on the conviction that their brains are incapable of absorbing the higher learning.

A Preface to Racial Understanding

We no longer believe with Dr. Van Evrie, an early physician writing on subjects dealing with the Negro, that because of the sloping angle of the Negro's head, as compared with the broad forehead of the white race, any attempt to educate the Negro would have the effect of destroying his center of gravity, rendering him incapable of walking upright.

Dr. S. A. Cartwright, of Louisiana, one of the most eminent of the physicians of seventy-five years ago, "demonstrated" that tuberculosis was "par excellence a disease of the white race, and that Negroes were incapable of it, because it was a disease of the master race and not of the slave race, known by an active hæmatosis, . . . by the energy of the intellect, vivid imagination, and an indomitable will and love of freedom." Early ethnologists held that the Negro affords a point at which man and beast most nearly approach each other. We no longer hear arguments regarding slavery as a natural state of the Negro, or that God inflicted subjection on women as a punishment for the sin of Eve, and on Negroes as punishment for the act of their ancestor, Ham, the son of Noah, who saw his father unattired and intoxicated. These convictions, once held with a passionate fervor, are for the most part museum pieces now, and it is difficult to believe that they were ever taken seriously.

Some Next Steps

It is not enough merely to wait watchfully for time's slow solution of social ills. Despite the vital rôle which economics plays in altering the sentiments of people, the personal factor in itself can also contribute to change and improvement in the economic basis of race problems. There are steps that can be taken immediately to correct old evils. The accumulation of these steps cannot fail to have their effect in remaking a tradition which controls so much of individual behavior.

Race relations, in an ultimate sense, are personal relations, and changes in relations may be expected to follow changed personal experiences. Despite the highly artificial character of many of the interracial gatherings, such gatherings do occasionally provide a first crude basis for meeting and getting acquainted.

There is a possibility that the race problem cannot be approached directly; that the best results may come not through formal agreements or through compromise between extreme positions, but through the unplanned by-products—the silent spread of friendships from casual contacts in other than a deliberate attempt to improve interracial friendship. It is certain that the spread of sentiments across the line of race can be salutary in individual cases. This assumes, however, a willingness to extend personally to those individuals of like interests who happen to differ in color the unstrained and unaffected graces of friendship, confidence and respect. Such spontaneous behavior, against the weight of tradition, cannot be expected to develop immediately on any large scale. For many years yet there will be usefulness in those programs which aim at making possible interracial contacts and from these contacts more thorough knowledge of the life of individuals in the separate groups.

A Preface to Racial Understanding

It is always difficult to reduce broad principles to concrete examples which are applicable over a wide range of specific situations. Nevertheless, it is one of the most insistent demands of groups and individuals who are motivated to some kind of social service, that they be provided specific suggestions of things to do, both as examples of what can be done and of what has been successfully accomplished. In the spirit of meeting this elementary demand, some practical interests and activities are noted.

It is necessary for the person who wishes to live and work intelligently in this challenging world, to know the present facts of race relations as these are expressed in the conventions, public practices, and the institutions of a community. Although an ambitious enterprise to undertake, it would be desirable to know something about the status of Negroes in relation to the industrial life of a given locality, the extent of mortality among them, and the degree to which they share the public provisions for the safeguarding of health. It would be useful to know something about their living conditions and the problem of finding good and beautiful homes; their record of crime and their treatment in the courts; their chances for recreation and wholesome amusement so essential to sound health and morals.

Increased knowledge of these local situations would doubtless lead to practical opportunities for constructive action and would give confidence and inspiration to any appeals that might be made for social justice. More exact information would help to remove the discussion of race from the universe of passion and sentimentality and give a truer perspective of the problem. If this is done, it is possible that the prevailing estimates of Negro character, mentality and morality, for example, would not have to rest so heavily upon the chance contact with a Negro domestic or even upon the crime reports which, almost alone among matters involving Negroes, have sufficient news value for publication in the daily press of the nation.

At the base of most of the social problems of the Negroes is the problem of work. Anyone who has given the least thought to this question must have observed that in the majority of cases the relation of Negroes to their employers, their opportunities for advancement and for an adequate wage, and often their relations with their white fellow workers, are very largely a matter of the attitude of employers. Human nature is not so unchangeable as it is usually assumed to be. As often as simple economic advantage, in the form of larger profits, has operated to set a pattern of tolerance in an industrial plant, just so often can the altered attitude of employers, as a result of the direct or indirect influence of respected citizens, bring about tolerance and a fair chance for Negro workers. Such a situation is not exclusively to the advantage of the Negroes so aided. Increased opportunity and earnings for them means increased buying power which, in turn, benefits business generally. Moreover, the lifting of the level of these Negro workers removes from white workers the penalty of competition which keeps their own living standards low.

A Preface to Racial Understanding

SOME SUCCESSFUL PRECEDENTS

Drawing upon the experiences of groups which have been successful in constructively altering the old patterns of race relations in various localities, these projects may be noted as types of possible and useful activity:

(1) Encouraging and aiding participation of Negro groups in the work of such organizations as the Parent-Teacher Associations, Young Men's Christian Associations, Young Women's Christian Associations, Leagues of Women Voters, Better Government Leagues, and similar organizations.

(2) Work with local administrative officials to secure the inclusion of Negroes in public provisions for education, health, recreation and work.

(3) Urging the broadening of the study of race problems in high school and college courses on sociology. In this connection should be mentioned the recommendation of field work projects, under competent direction, in the race or interracial field, and the use of white and Negro lecturers of high grade and sound understanding. The Phelps-Stokes Fellowship Studies at the University of Virginia and the University of Georgia are excellent examples of the usefulness of this type of special programs.

(4) Wide dissemination of literature which can help acquaint the general public with the correctable handicaps, as well as the striking evidences of the cultural development, of the Negro.

(5) Planning to insure the inclusion of Negroes in the cultural and economic advantages provided by the local community, whether these take the form of cooperatives or forums, musical programs or lectures.

(6) Making provision for the discussion of Negro welfare in local committees and an equitable share in the measures developed for the relief of the underprivileged.

(7) Cooperation with local librarians to the extent of recommending or securing for general reading a useful selection of books of poetry, novels and problem discussions dealing with the Negro.

(8) Work with organizations of labor to insure the inclusion of Negro workers, as sound economic and labor policy.

(9) Correction of injurious misstatements in the press.

(10) Active and pointed condemnation of such public crimes as mob violence and lynching, the prostitution of the courts in response to racial prejudice, and the economic exploitation of defenseless minorities, not merely in the interest of these minorities but in the interest of the morality of the nation itself.

(11) Encouragement of constructive experiences, such as musical programs, poetry reading, and folk plays which utilize Negro talent and racial experience.

(12) Creation of actual occasions for meeting, and the participation of Negro individuals in public affairs which have no specific relation to race problems as such.

This list could be continued, but only as evidences of the resourcefulness of individuals and groups of various communities, who have allowed their professed concern for social justice and a Christian way of life to find expression in practical action.

MUTUALITY OF OBLIGATIONS

The obligation to find a constructive basis for race relations does not lie wholly on one side of the line of race. In the desire of Negroes for improved status, for the same opportunities and privileges of American citizenship shared by the rest of the population, they also have an obligation for self-improvement and for an equal measure of service. To this end the work of the Federated Colored Women's Clubs, with a membership of more than a hundred thousand, and other similar organizations, has been notable and inspiring. Moreover, the experience of the Negro race itself over recent years has altered perspectives for them, and, on the deepening fringes of this advancing group, created new minds, new personalities, and new leadership for the years to follow.

Social and economic changes, and the constant pressure in our society for change, are occasions for the outbursts of racial prejudice. The wholesome desire for individual development and group progress conflicts all too frequently with an orthodox desire to keep the Negroes "in their place." In an age of rapid change this place is changing more rapidly than the orthodoxy. The margins of this cultural development of the Negro group are yet very uneven, but it can be said that their development has materially exceeded the external social devices for aiding their incorporation into American life.

The Conquest of Racial Prejudice

THE NEW NEGRO POINT OF VIEW

On the part of the emancipated Negro, there has been a loss of much of that sensitiveness which once blinded Negroes to themselves and to their surroundings at the same time that it injured their capacity for an accurate appraisal of themselves and their condition. There has been a more frank and less embarrassed acceptance of the fact of race and difference, but with the growing conviction that the difference has no vital and inherent meaning. There has been a willingness to seek out the hidden beauties of Negro life, and a result of this has been the stimulation of new curiosities among Negroes about themselves and the attachment of more charm to their own lives. There has been a more dispassionate recognition of the facts of Negro life and there have been certain admissions of racial weaknesses, based on the philosophy that if one is not truthful about his faults, which can be seen, he will not be believed when he speaks about his virtues, which are not always apparent on the surface. There is less apology for race and the purely social implications of race status. There is more confident self-expression and a deeper sharing of the whole culture of America.

The essence of the problem of race relations is change, and in this modern age change is constant, rapid and profound. Our physical world, our technological structure, our economic structure, our social institutions themselves are in constant process of change. Only in a stagnant society can we expect fixed and unalterable social relations, and a democracy is least of all political structures bound by unyielding conventions. Race problems may be expected to reflect the deep-lying and obscure changes in the society itself. New philosophies will appear as each new step of advance is accomplished, and, along with increased insights and understanding, new programs will be set up to implement these philosophies.

Of greatest concern to those who seek to deal justly and honestly in these affairs will be the assurance that their principles of action are as high as the example set by the faith which they profess. The whole history of mankind, says one philosopher, is the history of human endeavor to attain justice in this life. Indeed, it is the highest moral aim of men. A sound principle of action, thus, could well be: "Respect thy neighbor as thyself, even if thou canst not love him, and do not permit that he or thyself be treated with disrespect."

In the field of race relations, it is not so important that there should be envisaged exact solutions, for there will inevitably be differences of opinions. Solutions of situations for which there are so few precedents must necessarily be speculative, and speculation can often go too far afield. But it is important that there should be principles guiding these relationships, and that these principles should be high. Once Dr. Wallace Buttrick said of Booker T. Washington: "He early learned that one contributes best to the progress of human civilization by doing the next thing"; and along with this sound and practical philosophy goes another bit of wisdom from an old African proverb: "If you know well the beginning, the end will not trouble you much."

BIBLIOGRAPHICAL NOTES

For the student interested in the literature concerning the Negro there is a wide range of choice. The *Bibliography of the Negro in Africa and America,* compiled by Monroe N. Work and published in 1928 (H. W. Wilson Company), contains some seventeen thousand carefully selected and classified titles. There are at least six outstanding collections of "Afro-Americana" in the United States, of which the Schomburg Collection in the New York Public Library is perhaps best known and most complete. The Library of Congress published thirty years ago a list of references on the Negro question, which contained five hundred and twenty-two carefully selected references. And it is not unusual to find valuable Negro collections in state historical societies and university libraries. One of the best collections of Negro books in the South is that assembled at the Y.M.C.A. Graduate School in Nashville, Tennessee, by its president, Dr. W. D. Weatherford.

A pamphlet containing a carefully annotated list of books in this field may be secured from the New York Public Library, Circulation Office, 42d Street and Fifth Avenue, New York City. The title is *The Negro: A Selected Bibliography* (1935); price 10 cents.

Interest in the Negro has been growing in recent years, and volumes dealing with his problems are in demand, not simply because they deal with the Negro, but because Negro life presents illuminating aspects of American life generally. It will be useful, however, to the reader who wishes to pursue his reading further to have at hand a brief selected bibliography.

Bibliographical Notes

HISTORY

Carter G. Woodson's *The Negro in Our History* (Associated Publishers, 1928, $3.25) could well be used as a text in courses in Negro history. It is the most complete story available of the part played by Negroes in American history, and represents the work of a trained and experienced historian. The same author's *History of the Negro Church* (Associated Publishers, 1921, $2.50) is an excellent and illuminating historical research. Benjamin Brawley gives, in *The Social History of the American Negro* (The Macmillan Company, 1921, $4.00), an account of what has happened to America because of the Negro's presence here. *The Negro*, by W. E. Burghardt DuBois (Henry Holt and Company, 1915, $1.00), does much to dispel the idea that the Negro has had no past and "that his normal condition is that of subordination and slavery." In *Black Reconstruction* (Harcourt, Brace and Company, 1935, $4.50) the same author seeks, through well documented material, to interpret the period in American history between 1860 and 1880, with special reference to the efforts and experiences of Negroes. An authoritative survey of the African backgrounds of Negroes, the American slave system and its aftermath, and the educational, social and religious progress of Negroes since emancipation is found in *The Story of the American Negro*, by Ina C. Brown (Friendship Press, 1936, $1.00).

A general picture of the New York Negro from the early seventeenth century until the present is given in James Weldon Johnson's *Black Manhattan* (Alfred A. Knopf, 1930, $3.00). The reader interested in the beginnings of Negro education will find an excellent account of the efforts made to educate Negroes during the days of slavery in *The Education of the Negro Prior to 1861* (Associated Publishers, $2.50), by Carter G. Woodson. The same author, in a recent volume, *The Mis-Education of the Negro* (Associated Publishers, 1933, $2.00), considers the modern education of the Negro as conforming to the needs of those who oppress him rather than suited to the Negro himself.

RACE AND CULTURE

Thomas R. Garth's *Race Psychology* (McGraw-Hill Book Company, 1931, $2.50) is an attempt to answer the question whether or not racial differences in mental traits exist. This volume presents an account of all scientific studies and findings in this field from 1881. An anthropometric discussion of the Negro, significant for both anthropologists and sociologists, may be found in Melville J. Herskovits's *The American Negro* (Alfred A. Knopf, 1928, $1.75). Another authoritatively scientific treatment of the material dealing with race differences will be found in *Race Differences,* by Otto Klineberg (Harper and Brothers, 1935, $2.50). Dr. Paul Radin in *The Racial Myth* (McGraw-Hill Book Company, 1934, $1.50) shows the growth of the myth of racial superiority from earliest times, and interprets this growth in nationalistic and racial terms.

Books dealing with problems of race and racial adjustment have been appearing recently. The history, philosophy, program and techniques of ten national interracial agencies are outlined in *Negro-White Adjustment,* by Paul E. Baker (Association Press, 1934, $3.00). For a discussion of the relation and contribution of one racial element to the body politic as a whole, *The Gift of Black Folk,* by W. E. Burghardt DuBois (Associated Publishers, 1924, $2.00) will be found most useful. Bruno Lasker in *Race Attitudes in Children* (Henry Holt and Company, 1929, $4.00) outlines the forms which race attitudes take in children and the ways in which they express themselves. For a discussion of studies of the group mind and of group conflicts, with each group seeking to assert its will to power over other groups, Herbert A. Miller's *Races, Nations and Classes* (J. B. Lippincott Company, 1924, $2.00) will prove enlightening. *Race Relations,* by W. D.

Bibliographical Notes

Weatherford and Charles S. Johnson (D. C. Heath and Company, 1934, $3.20), attempts a thorough study of the "Negro problem," in the light of the facts and conditions involved.

CONTEMPORARY SOCIAL PROBLEMS

An excellent introduction to the study of the race problem in America is Edwin R. Embree's *Brown America* (Friendship Press, 1936, special edition, $1.25), which touches briefly upon the beginnings of the Negro in America and describes the race's cultural gifts to the nation through folk art, music and the fine arts. *The American Race Problem,* by Edward B. Reuter (T. Y. Crowell Company, 1927, $2.75), covers such phases of the life of the Negro as health, economic status, and crime, with brief, clear summaries of salient facts that have been collected in connection with each subject. Robert Russa Moton, principal emeritus of Tuskegee Institute, in *What the Negro Thinks* (Doubleday, Doran and Company, 1929, $2.00), presents a clear-cut record of the opinions of a representative section of the Negro race as it views American life "with its rules of living set up by white men," and of the Negro's "success in making a contribution to the whole of American life in spite of the obstacles placed in his way." *The Negro in American Civilization,* by Charles S. Johnson (Henry Holt and Company, 1930, $4.00), deals with the Negro in agriculture and industry, Negro health and housing, Negro education and educability, citizenship and law observance, and certain subtle and intractable problems of race relations. In *Negro Americans, What Now?* (The Viking Press, 1934, $1.25), James Weldon Johnson outlines the racial system existing today, and offers suggestions of ways which may lead out. Donald R. Young, in *American Minority Peoples* (Harper and Brothers, 1932, $3.50), analyzes the status of various minority groups in American life, including the Negro, the Indian, the Jew, and various immigrant groups. It is a most important volume because of its objec-

Bibliographical Notes

tive treatment of problems normally regarded as racial, but which are merely characteristic of minority group status.

Among the books dealing with contemporary social problems are several extremely important ones which treat special topics more exhaustively than those just mentioned. Of these the following are to be noted: *The Education of the Negro in the American Social Order,* by Horace Mann Bond (Prentice-Hall, Inc., 1934, $2.75); *The Negro Family in Chicago,* by E. Franklin Frazier (University of Chicago Press, 1932, $3.00); *The Southern Urban Negro as a Consumer,* by Paul K. Edwards (Prentice-Hall, Inc., 1932, $5.00); *Negro Politicians,* by Harold F. Gosnell (University of Chicago Press, 1935, $3.50); *The Negro Peasant Turns Cityward,* by Louise Venable Kennedy (Columbia University Press, 1930, $4.25); *The Mobility of the Negro,* by Edward E. Lewis (Columbia University Press, 1931, $2.25); and *Negro Problems in Cities,* by T. J. Woofter (Harper and Brothers, 1928, $1.75). The last three titles have particular reference to the migration of Negroes.

A well rounded picture of the growth of the Negro church is presented in the volume by Benjamin E. Mays and J. W. Nicholson, *The Negro's Church* (Harper and Brothers, 1933, $2.00). *The Trend of the Races,* a volume prepared by George E. Haynes for the Missionary Education Movement and the Council of Women for Home Missions in 1922 (50 cents) will be found useful for its information and instructive point of view. Dr. J. H. Oldham's *Christianity and the Race Problem* (Association Press, 1924, paper, $1.00) continues an outstanding work of an internationally known Christian student on a subject of mounting concern. A briefer but no less interesting treatment of the theme of religion in race relations will be found in Robert E. Speer's *Of One Blood* (Missionary Education Movement and Council of Women for Home Missions, 1924, 25 cents).

A clear dissection of the social anomaly of the lynchings of

197

1930, presented with observations and conclusions, will be found in *The Tragedy of Lynching,* by Arthur F. Raper (University of North Carolina Press, 1933, $2.50); while Walter F. White, in *Rope and Faggot* (Alfred A. Knopf, 1929, $3.00), analyzes the public mind, the theories of inferiority and superiority, the economic status and the religious ideas which he believes play a part in mob violence.

THE NEGRO IN INDUSTRY AND AGRICULTURE

The books dealing with Negro economic status demand special attention. Abram L. Harris and Sterling D. Spero (a white and Negro collaboration in authorship) in *The Black Worker* (Columbia University Press, 1931, $4.50) set forth the Negro as a worker from conditions of slavery to the present day, showing the interaction of such factors as race prejudice, trade union politics and structure, and the conditions of the labor market. Beginning with slave labor in colonial times Charles H. Wesley reviews, chronologically, in *Negro Labor in the United States, 1850-1925* (Vanguard Press, 1927, 50 cents), the story of Negro labor, economic progress and the spread of industrialism among Negro Americans. *The Negro Wage Earner,* by Lorenzo J. Greene and Carter G. Woodson (Association for the Study of Negro Life and History, 1930, $3.25), is a study of the industrial struggle of the Negro from 1890 to 1930. Ira De A. Reid's *Negro Membership in American Labor Unions* (National Urban League, 1930, paper, $1.00) is a presentation of most valuable factual material dealing with the formal aspects of the Negro in relation to labor organizations. While treating all minority groups, special emphasis is placed upon the Negro in Herman Feldman's *Racial Factors in American Industry* (Harper and Brothers, 1931, $4.00), depicting employment handicaps and plant policies, and describing the application of management technique to racial problems and adjustments. Charles S. Johnson's *Shadow of the Plantation* (University of

Bibliographical Notes

Chicago Press, 1934, $2.50) is a study of the plantation from the inside, and of Negro personality changes under conditions of race and culture in a Southern community. This study is also in part an interpretation of the present agricultural problem in the South through an analysis of the existing economic system. Findings and conclusions regarding cotton tenancy in the Southern cotton belt appear in *The Collapse of Cotton Tenancy,* by Charles S. Johnson, Edwin R. Embree and W. W. Alexander (University of North Carolina Press, 1935, $1.00). In *The Rural Negro* (Association for the Study of Negro Life and History, 1930, $2.50), Carter G. Woodson sets forth how and where the six and a half million rural Negroes make a living, spend their leisure, go to church, and keep alive amid social and economic irregularities which engulf them on every side.

BIOGRAPHY

The biographical literature offers an interesting variety of personal stories which permit insight into Negro life and experience. There is a group of no less than one hundred and fifty narratives of slaves and ex-slaves, many of which were written by the slaves themselves and others by abolitionists, who hoped thereby to advance the cause of freedom. Outstanding among these is the *Life and Times of Frederick Douglass* (DeWolfe and Fiske Company) written by Douglass himself and published in 1892 as an enlargement of the same author's book *My Bondage and My Freedom.* The most widely read of all such literature is Booker T. Washington's *Up from Slavery* (Doubleday, Page and Company, 1900), which has been translated into seventy languages. It is the story of a slave who became one of America's foremost citizens and educators. James Weldon Johnson's *Along This Way* (The Viking Press, 1933, $3.50) is best described by Carl Van Doren as "a book any man might be proud to have written about a life any man might be proud to have lived." These three volumes mark, in an

Bibliographical Notes

important sense, three major periods in the career of the Negro race in America.

There are many volumes of brief biographical sketches. Hallie Q. Brown published privately in 1926 *Homespun Heroines* (Wilberforce, Ohio), a collection of biographies of fifty-four Negro women, assembling an array of interesting information hitherto little known about women in various fields of successful work. Ralph W. Bullock's *In Spite of Handicaps* (Association Press, 1927, $2.00) carries sketches of eighteen contemporary American Negroes who have succeeded in business, professional and artistic pursuits. Georgina A. Gollock, an English writer, in *Sons of Africa* (Friendship Press, 1928, 75 cents) has drawn together a valuable collection of biographies of outstanding leaders, including African kings and chiefs of pre-modern times and living native leaders, while her *Daughters of Africa* (Longmans, Green and Company, 1932, $1.00) gives short sketches of native African women. The former is interesting particularly for the light it throws on African leaders who have figured conspicuously in recent cultural changes in Africa.

Sadie I. Daniel's *Women Builders* (Associated Publishers, 1931, $2.00) is a readable collection of biographies of contemporary Negro women. *For Freedom,* by Arthur Fauset (Franklin Publishing Company, 1927, $1.50), a small volume designed for high schools, is the story of Negro heroes from African days to the present. Mary White Ovington's *Portraits in Color* (The Viking Press, 1927, $2.00) covers a widely assorted group of representative Negroes, including a biologist, a singer, a botanist, and a social worker, and provides an intimate portrayal of these Negroes. *Twelve Negro Americans,* by Mary Jenness (Friendship Press, 1936, $1.00), consists of short sketches of personal achievement by Negroes in a variety of fields.

For those interested in the life experience of a very brilliant African Negro whose religious work left a deep mark on his

Bibliographical Notes

people, Edwin W. Smith's *Aggrey of Africa* (Friendship Press, 1936, special edition, $1.00) will prove most helpful and inspiring.

ANTHOLOGIES

Since many of the recent Negro literary publications are referred to in the text, it is unnecessary to repeat the titles here. Readers may find it useful, however, to have at hand references to a few notable anthologies of Negro literature. In *The New Negro* (Albert and Charles Boni, 1925, $5.00) Alain Locke presents a varied and vivid symposium of the best and most inclusive work of the contemporary Negro. James Weldon Johnson's *The Book of American Negro Poetry* (Harcourt, Brace and Company, 1931, revised edition, $2.00), while an anthology of contemporary Negro poetry, is introduced by an essay which presents the case for the Negro's capacity for making original contributions to American art and literature. For a volume giving fuller representation to the older poets, the *Anthology of Verse by American Negroes,* by Newman Ivey White and Walter Clinton Jackson (Duke University Press, 1924, $2.00), is suggested. Victor F. Calverton's *An Anthology of American Negro Literature* (The Modern Library, 1929, 95 cents) presents a useful picture of the intellectual development of the American Negro, through short stories, excerpts from novels, essays, spirituals, poetry and music. *Caroling Dusk* (Harper and Brothers, 1927, $2.50), edited by Countee Cullen, is an anthology of the poetry of the younger Negro writers, by one of the most accomplished and best known of that group. It carries short biographical sketches of each contributing poet.

INDEX

Africa, changes in, 7; colonial policies in, 15-16; cultures of, 5; education in, 16; European expansion in, 13-14; labor supply of, 22

African Reconstruction Association, 174

Agencies for interracial cooperation, 164-72

Agriculture Adjustment Administration, 37

Alexander, Virginia, 126-29

Alexander, W. W., 168

Allen, Floyd P., 49

Allen, Richard, 152-53

American Baptist Home Missionary Society, educational work of, 80

American Missionary Association, 80; in education, 67, 76, 148

Ames, Jessie Daniel, 181

Armstrong, Samuel E., 76

Art, Negro, 111-12

Ayllón, Lucas Vásquez de, 18

Ballagh, J. C., 21

Banneker, Benjamin, 91, 104

Baptists, 80, 145-46; on slavery, 153

Barrow, Reverend David, 145-46

Benezet, Anthony, 151

Blair, Henry, 91

Bond, Horace Mann, 182

Bontemps, Arna, 111

Bousfield, Maudelle Brown, 131-33

Brown, Charlotte Hawkins, 113-20

Brown, Sterling, 109

Carman, Reverend Joshua, 146

Cartwright, Samuel A., 184

Catholic Board for Mission Work among Colored People, 172

Chavis, John, 24

Chesnutt, Charles W., 107

Christianity among slaves, 100-1

Church of England, 144

Churches, and interracial cooperation, 157-59; attitude toward slavery of, colonial, 143-48; contributions of, to Negro education, 68-69, 79-81, 148-49; modern attitude toward Negroes of, 147-48; social and evangelistic activities of, 148-51; see also Missions

Code Noir, 20

Colonization schemes, 23-24, 162-63, 172-73, 174

Commission on Interracial Cooperation, 165, 168-69, 181

Cortez, 18

Cotton, areas, 32; culture, 25; gin, 24; market, 36; operators, 30; picker, 37; prices, 31; production, 26; tenant, 33-35

Cullen, Countee, 109

Daniel, William A., 155

Davis, Jefferson, 91

Davis, John W., 82

Delaney, Martin, 75

De Soto, 17

Dew, Thomas R., 25

203

Index

Index

Index

206